The BlackBerry® Diaries

ADVENTURES IN MODERN MOTHERHOOD

Kathy Buckworth

KEY PORTER BOOKS

Library and Archives Canada Cataloguing in Publication

Buckworth, Kathy
    The BlackBerry diaries : adventures in modern motherhood / Kathy Buckworth.

ISBN 978-1-55470-154-4

1. Mothers—Humor. 2. Parenting—Humor. 3. Technology—Humor. I. Title.

HQ759.B81 2009   306.874'3   C2008-906633-2

ONTARIO ARTS COUNCIL
CONSEIL DES ARTS DE L'ONTARIO

The publisher gratefully acknowledges the support of the Canada Council for the Arts
and the Ontario Arts Council for its publishing program. We acknowledge the support
of the Government of Ontario through the Ontario Media Development Corporation's
Ontario Book Initiative.

We acknowledge the financial support of the Government of Canada through the Book
Publishing Industry Development Program (BPIDP) for our publishing activities.

BlackBerry®, RIM®, Research In Motion®, and related trademarks, names and logos are
the property of Research In Motion Limited and are registered and/or used in the U.S.
and countries around the world.

Key Porter Books Limited
Six Adelaide Street East, Tenth Floor
Toronto, Ontario
Canada M5C 1H6

www.keyporter.com

Text design and formatting: Marijke Friesen

Printed and bound in Canada

09 10 11 12 13 5 4 3 2 1

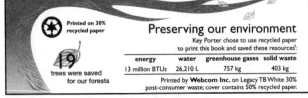

Printed on 30%
recycled paper

Preserving our environment

Key Porter chose to use recycled paper
to print this book and saved these resources[1]:

energy	water	greenhouse gases	solid waste
13 million BTUs	26,210 L	757 kg	403 kg

19 trees were saved for our forests

Printed by **Webcom Inc.** on Legacy TB White 30%
post-consumer waste; cover contains 50% recycled paper.

FSC

Mixed Sources
Product group from well-managed
forests, controlled sources and
recycled wood or fiber

Cert no. SW-COC-002358
www.fsc.org
© 1996 Forest Stewardship Council

[1]Estimates were made using the Environmental Defense Paper Calculator.

The BlackBerry® Diaries

As always, to my BlackBerry® Partner in Crime, Steve, and the four main reasons I need to escape to the virtual world; my children Victoria, Alexander, Bridget, and Nicholas . . . before flying back to reality once more.

Acknowledgements

My wish for this book is to make people laugh. At me, with me, whatever. So, I'd like to acknowledge some of the people (and things) that are making me laugh right now: my own reflection at yoga class; my Sherwood Forrest girlfriends when they say, "Oh, I can only stay for one drink;" teachers who expect me to know where we are in the curriculum; cheese in a can; anyone who thinks they're fun to be around; the name Seamus; my book club pals who say, "No, your stuff is really good, too;" Jeff, Scott, Robbie, Jamie and Robyn in full moon; and men whose only comeback is, "You're such a girl!"

There are also many people who make me smile—and luckily for me, four of them live in my house. My beautiful and fashion-conscious daughter Victoria ("Mom are you going to wear that? I'm just asking."); my broody and exponentially growing son Alexander (who proves that the smart-ass apple doesn't fall far from the sarcastic tree); my gorgeous, athletic and hockey-mad daughter Bridget ("Mmmm, I love the smell of the arena!"); and finally my Windex-obsessed son Nicholas and his startling inventiveness ("I only wore one pair of underwear all week and you never noticed!"). For the record, I noticed.

Special thanks and pleas for forgiveness as well to my husband Steve Webster (yes, as you stated, in your defence, you do take out the garbage). And, as always, my chief editor and Editor-in-Chief, Linda Pruessen, and my diligent agent, Carolyn Swayze.

And I need to mention how proud I am that a Canadian company invented the BlackBerry. Well done, eh.

Preface:
Allow Me to Explain Myself

As a thoroughly Modern Mother, what I love most about my BlackBerry smartphone is that it allows me to maintain the façade of dedicated writer, knowledgeable public speaker, and little known but professionally made-up television personality while simultaneously living the perilous life of the harried, time-starved, harassed, and generally cranky mom. Some of my best career wins have been communicated to me over my BlackBerry smartphone, in less than ideal circumstances. To whit: the call I took from my agent, letting me know that I was being offered a book deal on *Journey to the Darkside: Supermom Goes Home*, came while I was standing in line at the grocery store, buying lice shampoo. I had to pretend not to care about the grossed out look on the cashier's face (as she simultaneously scanned my purchase and backed up a good 14 inches so as not to be infested) while also wanting to grab her and yell, "I have a book deal! You should care!" I'm sure she thought I was insane—some crazy woman grinning and bouncing on her feet at the prospect of delousing as an afternoon's entertainment.

My point is this: the BlackBerry smartphone fits my lifestyle. It defines my lifestyle. And it will get you, too.

Let the adventure begin.

Introduction

When I started to write this book, I had a crazy idea. I was going to tap out the entire thing out on my handheld—just for fun and effect. That lasted about two minutes until I realized that there is more to being a Modern Mother than clicking away on my new best friend. This became imminently clear as I attempted to jostle a screaming 4-year-old off my left foot, wave frantically at my 13-year-old son to stop shaking the arena's pop machine, raise a finger to my sullen teen daughter in the universal "just a minute" signal, and show enthusiasm for my 7-year-old daughter's hockey skills with just my eyes. That's when I had the big revelation: my BlackBerry had become my fifth child—and the perfect complement to the Modern Motherhood world in which I live.

While previous generations of moms have certainly faced bigger challenges (say, the plague, or no electricity), this age has its own obstacles to overcome. Thankfully, we have "aids" to help us along our path of birthing the children, raising the children, and then getting said frigging children out the front door so we can resume our so-called real lives. The BlackBerry is the best of those aids. It allows me to stay linked to a world outside of Play-Doh, tantrums, and the judgment that comes from other challenged Modern Mothers.

For example, my 4-year-old son Nicholas is currently holding his bottom and telling me that he thinks something might have snuck out. I have wrested myself away from the computer, secure in the knowledge that I can take my email with me on my belt. I might need it, after all, to block out the images of the bathroom in front of me (yes, if I'm lucky whatever has "snuck out" is actually in the bathroom). You get what I'm saying. Modern Moms have to "be in the moment" physically, but sometimes—in order to make it through the day with our sanity intact—it is necessary to find distractions to take us away from the literal day-to-day shit with which we are constantly faced.[*]

And so, welcome to my blog. Or I guess it's more like a plog (given that blog is short for web-log and this one is on paper). *The BlackBerry Diaries: Adventures in Modern Motherhood* will take you on a journey through the perils of parenting in our time. It's all about balance—something with which Modern Mothers are intimately familiar. If you have a BlackBerry, you're already with me on this. If you haven't yet succumbed, the device will appear on the top of your Christmas list next year, right next to the membership in the Wine of the Month club.

[*] For those of you who are curious about what exactly was "stuck," apparently it was a "poo ball." Luckily, it hasn't actually appeared, so it's all good from where I'm standing.

Handy Definitions for the BlackBerry Smartphone Owner

BlackBerry smartphone: Either you have one or you want one. Get one and read on.

RIM (Research In Motion): They made the BlackBerry smartphone. To help you keep up with your Life In Motion.

BBSP: Abbreviation of the above-mentioned moniker "BlackBerry smartphone," deployed by this writer in order to save on typeset and ink costs.

BB: Even shorter version. That ink isn't getting any cheaper as we sit here.

Seamus: My own personal nickname for my own personal BlackBerry smartphone. A crafty and subtle writer's trick to infer that the device has become my fifth child. Also a diversionary tactic to avoid using the proper and annoying terminology of "BlackBerry smartphone."

BlackBerry: Acts as a diversion from whining children, nagging spouses, annoying housework, interfering neighbours, making small talk to strangers and more!

Luddite: Any individual who does not own or condone the use of the above.

Berry-envy: Condition that strikes individuals who are not willing or able to join the BBSP Revolution. Manifests itself in platitudes such as "I refuse to get one of those leashes," "I'm trying to simplify my life," or "They're so obnoxious . . . no one needs one."

Smackberry: The sound of two BB hitting as spouses greet each other with a quick hug or kiss.

Aaackberry: The horrible realization that you have left your house without your little friend.

Braxberry: Derived from the term "Braxton Hicks," which anyone who has been pregnant knows is a pseudo-contraction that feels like the real thing. Describes the phantom vibration phenomenon that occurs even when one is not wearing the handheld device.

Gasp-berrying: Receiving an alarming email that you have surreptitiously looked at when you are not supposed to be looking (at, say, your daughter's dance competition, while in conversation with your mother-in-law, in bed).

Mask-berrying: Pretending you don't use it when out with your more "granola"-type friends. "Oh yes, I have one—damn office—but I only use it for emergencies."

Brag-berrying: Assuming you are the only person in the world to be at the constant beck and call of your electronic leader. "It goes off non-stop. Sometimes the buzzing drives everyone around me nuts! But what am I supposed to do?"

Handy Definitions for the Toddler Owner

Blarching: The lurching, arching, and general squirming about that a toddler performs when being unjustly and involuntarily put into a stringent torturous device known as the "car seat." Can also be activated by the common shopping cart.

Sh-Boot: The art of holding onto a convenient staircase, tippy hall table or even more unstable parent, while simultaneously shaking one leg with violent thrusts until a constrictive and rubberized containment unit known as a rain boot is ejected from the blighted foot to land squarely in the face of an innocent bystander or bewildered family pet.

Entoddlerment: The unshakable belief instilled in all small children that not only does the credo "my way or the highway" hold true, but that "my way" is best performed after the activity in question has already been performed to resounding success by a clueless caregiver. Examples: slipping on Velcro runners, unwrapping cheese string things, and choosing underwear.

Ambi-shoe-drous: The ability (and suspected preference) of toddlers to wear and walk in shoes and boots placed with right on left, and left on right. (P.S. They don't care if they look silly—it feels fine! Me do it!)

Magnetoddler: The unexplained yet totally provable theory that every tiny dust and dirt particle circling in the immediate area of a small child will be sucked into the palms, creases, and folds of their chubby little hands.

Expeleration: The release of the accumulated materials from Magnetoddler. This occurs only when the toddler is brought into contact with freshly washed windows, white linen skirts, elderly relatives' cream coloured shag carpets or pale yellow brushed-suede couches.

Snottler: A toddler with a continuous supply of dischargeable materials from the nasal cavities. The stream (or boulders, depending) may be stemmed only by the insertion of same child's magnetoddlerized finger. Affects approximately 99% of the toddler population.

Explodderation: The red face, clenched fists, stamping feet, and shriek of rage that is characteristic of all small children upon the unexpected and totally infuriating discovery that life is, in fact, "not fair." A similar reaction can be discovered while viewing grown men watch their favourite sports team or children's Triple A hockey team lose in a game where the referee is clearly a biased idiot.

The BlackBerry® Diaries

December 25
The Birth of a New Life:
My BlackBerry Smartphone Awaits

I have only two hands, and one of them is usually holding a glass of chardonnay. But not today. Today I'm holding a brand spanking new piece of heaven—my very own BlackBerry smartphone! Oh, how I have longed for one. This is the piece of technology that will transform my life. I will be able to stay on top of emails, track personal and professional appointments, stay "in the loop" and "on the page" and all without turning over my entire life to this electronic device, but simply using it as an effective Mommy Management tool. I just know it! Why? No, I'm not a Bay Street banker, hot shot lawyer, media executive or overinflated academic. I'm a writer. And I have four children. In case you don't fit into either one of these categories, I need to explain that they are often mutually exclusive professions locked in a battle for co-existence. At least until now. Now I have my hands on this little beauty, which will allow me to be completely organized, stay on top of things, receive messages from everyone who needs to reach me—voice or email—and keep me connected with everyone and everything I hold dear. And I will not let it take over my life, like so many of my over-the-top friends have done.

I will use it; it will not use me. Now, where's that chardonnay?

Tags: BlackBerry smartphone. Kids. Heaven.

January 2
It Occurs to Me

BBSPs and children share many of the same ownership challenges, and many of the same moments of joy and desperation. But being a parent, particularly a Modern Mother, means facing quite a few obstacles and life-decision moments. Like whether or not it is worth the effort to leave the discount shoe store and drive across town to the specialty soccer shoe retailer where your amazing athletic progeny can buy a pair of overpriced trendy cleats that will last for precisely one month—wait, are they even open at this hour? Well, let's just pull out Seamus (remember this is my BlackBerry smartphone, not a reference to a technically inclined child or a body part) and see! Start Googling!

Yes, this may just be your best Parenting Aid in a world gone Parental Control mad. What would that perfect Mom down the street do? Now you can find out in moments. If you want to.

(Now can I have that endorsement cheque, Mr. Balsillie? I know lots of Moms; I can even put up a flyer in the school office on how to fundraise for one's own BB.)

Tags: Parenting. Control. Myth.

January 4
Misery Loves Company

So far it's been a lovely honeymoon with my new friend . . . mostly. As with all relationships, the bloom is fading from the rose as I discover my partner's quirks and character traits at close range; there is often a fine line between love and hate.

My little electronic companion (Seamus, pay attention!) insists on buzzing, beeping, and vibrating at an ever-increasing pace (or, even more frustrating . . . not working at all), particularly when I'm dealing with a tantrummy toddler. Now I know that they are often referred to as an "electronic leash," but I find this kind of surprising. A "leash" implies that you are a slave or dog of some kind, and totally unable to disconnect yourself from your master. Although this *is* actually true for the parents of a toddler, in the case of the BBSP, I am left to ponder exactly who the master is—work? boss? nagging spouse? The RIM people themselves? Why not just turn the damn thing off every once in a while? With rumours and innuendo like this, I fear I'll never be able to convert new users (although the Church of Scientology is still attracting new folk, so the world is a nutty place).

It's only natural that I'll try to bring new users into my new BBSP world. As a parent, after all, I occasionally try to convince those quiet, tidy, organized people of the world (yes, the childless) to have their own offspring so they can understand what my world is really like. It's not nice of me, really. These people think they've had a hard weekend if the Starbucks barista got their latte order wrong. Hello, you're in the Starbucks getting a latte on the weekend, not in a cold hockey arena or manic indoor playground, so I'm really not interested in hearing about your tragedy, okay? Walk a mile in my child-friendly shoes and send me an email, if you can find the time.

Tags: Non-believers. Baristas.

January 7
Toddlers and Berries and Zombies, Oh My!

One week into my BB ownership, it's become obvious to me that users, like parents, have a huge learning curve. It's occurred to me that much of this has to do with our expectations. Think about it. No one can truly explain what it's like to have a real, live baby in your house, and no one could really describe the transformative moment when I held that adorable little thing in my arms (okay, fingers) for the first time. I have never met anyone who says, "Yeah, I got one last month, but I rarely turn it on. I just can't get into it." It's as unlikely as hearing a new parent say, "Yeah, we brought the baby home from the hospital last month, but honestly, we forget it's there sometimes." Don't get me wrong. There are times when I would love to be able to ignore the fact that my BlackBerry is sitting in my purse, or on my belt, just waiting for me to turn it on and find out what I've been missing. But I am strong enough to resist and pay attention to the hockey practice, the violin recital . . . even the dinner-time dialogue. What, I'm a loser or something?

So, in the interest of full disclosure, I've been thinking about how to advise the newbies.

I'll deal with the virgin user first. There are people out there who are planning on getting a Blackberry. So far, so good. But then they go and alarm themselves and others by stating that they're actually a little bit worried about signing up. I understand that this type of hesitation is especially prevalent among those who have read the media reports about users becoming totally addicted. Bah. These virgins are afraid that they, too, will be taken over, and disappear, zombie-like, into the technological void. This may happen. What may also happen is that they will—I don't know—join the new millennium? There are some people who should *never* get a BBSP, and I now believe they share the following characteristics:

- A small social network (and you know what they say about people with a small social network . . .).
- Ownership of at least one pair of Birkenstocks, and a favourite pair of socks that goes with them.
- Six different types of granola in their cupboard, right now.
- More likely to strap on a "water bottle belt" or a fanny pack than to attach the patron saint of technology and communication (the BB, you idiot).
- A huge interest in the local newspaper, because really, who needs to know what goes on in the big bad world. (Prone to saying "I find the news so depressing!" Duh.)
- A pair of zip-off pants (this could apply to young children, or men and women who hate to admit to themselves that they are not camping all the time).
- Refers to the portable telephone, microwave oven, DVD player, and answering machines as "those newfangled things."
- Thinks that "Bluetooth" is the unfortunate result of a denture wearer eating blueberries.
- Drives a pickup truck, owns a gun, refers to "going into the city," and uses the term "youse guys."

There are also some people who really should think twice about having children. For instance, people who:

- Do not enjoy picking up the same 17 little cars every single day and putting them back in the "handy" carrying case, making sure to use the same slots (to avoid the wrath of the wronged toddler).

• Love starting a sentence, talking through the sentence, and finishing the sentence all without having to yell "take that out of your underwear right now" and then carry on as if nothing unusual has just transpired.

• Prefer their white sofa to stay white. You have a white sofa and you're expecting? Call Adoption Services; it's not too late.

• Find it unreasonable to allow a toddler to take off a perfectly placed winter boot, then put it back on in exactly the same way, because they have to.

• Get upset about little people who answer "No" to the question "Do you need to go pee?" but have an instant reversal of opinion once the snowsuit is on, the boots are in place, and the organ in question is tightly fastened into a car seat.

• Enjoy bruise-less shins.

A word to the wise (or the birth-control challenged): Not everyone is cut out to be a parent, period, but being the parent of a toddler draws on negotiation skills and reserves of patience only world and religious leaders should be expected to possess. The constant attention-seeking, questioning, and incessant noise is equalled only by ... well ... my overactive Seamus. Scared yet?

One more thing I've discovered—make sure you choose the BlackBerry that is right for you. As with dogs, I think that one's BB takes on the personality of its owner. For instance, my husband's is blue and kind of cold steel and goes with Bay Street, while mine is black and shiny and matches most of my shoes.

Choose wisely.

Tags: Virgins. Freaks. Geeks.

January 15
The Horror, the Horror!

The unthinkable just happened. The entire North American land mass is in the midst of a BB "lockdown." The network is completely disabled. I'm watching the news in total disbelief as reporters interview users about their reaction to such a disastrous turn of events. It is absolutely staggering to listen to people state that they are glad their BB isn't functioning, as it will "allow them to get some work done." Frankly, I can't be the only person who is worried about sitting through a hockey game or a school council meeting without one. Yes, you're right—I'd never be at the school council meeting in the first place. The hockey, I paid for.

First of all, turn the damn thing off if it's distracting you. Second, um, perhaps it is just possible that sending emails relating to work is actually, erm, work? These people truly haven't grasped the BB concept and need to rethink their commitment to our world. They *should* be freaking out—freaks.

I, for one, know that I will be able to get through the school council meeting this afternoon without having the comfort of my real-world counterparts available to me at the touch of a button. (Besides, they're bound to have the network up again within minutes, aren't they? Other people will be getting really antsy about this.)

Tags: Apocalypse. Paralysis. Duh.

January 23
Some Things Never Change

While I'd like to believe women today are living in a new era—of parenting, womanhood, wifedom, and mothering—the sad truth is that most of the time I find myself engaging in exactly the same conversations that have been going on since the dawn of time. Yes, I wish my husband would put the dishes in the dishwasher; yes, it is very hard to fit in time for exercise; and yes, children are a) annoying, b) still learning how to walk, talk, sleep, and eat, and c) boring to listen to other people talk about.

Sometimes, I think it would be worthwhile to put together an audio tape of the conversations you know you're going to have during the first 18 years of your child's life. It would save you time and effort, and allow listeners to tune in only should they feel the need. Topics could include:

I didn't know how hard it would be to get a good night's sleep: From infancy through teething, bedwetting, nightmares, snoring, sleepwalking, sleep talking, late-night hockey games, waiting up for babysitters to return, and exam cramming, your children will keep you awake from before they are born right until they leave the nest. (Remember being pregnant and trying to sleep? Or trying to get pregnant and trying to sleep? Or even thinking you're pregnant when you don't want to be pregnant and trying to sleep?)

Driving to and from lessons: Yes, we all do it, and yes, it is boring as hell. In fact, the only thing more boring than the driving itself is listening to someone recount the time they have spent in the car, where they are going, why they are going (because Johnny is a gymnastics prodigy, that's why!), what they ate, how much time they wasted, how spectacular the child in question was at hockey/dance/karate/swimming, and why they love it all so. Come to think of it, scratch this topic from the list and just stop talking about it.

Fights between other women: How fun is it to talk about the big tussle in which two female friends are engaged? Very. How fun is it to listen to it, particularly if you don't even know the women who are fighting? About as fun as watching your 7-year-old's soccer practice. (Note: if you find the soccer practice exciting, you fall into the trap laid out in the item above. Do us all a favour and stop talking about it.) Still, we love to rehash the "She said/she said" conversations to make sure every little innuendo has been eked out. Here's a thought: Maybe when she said "Your hair looks nice," that's what she really meant.

My husband is mostly a total buffoon: Well, surprise, surprise, and aren't they all (except the ones who are gay and trying just a little harder). No, they don't know how to do laundry, and no, they haven't been in a grocery store for 17 years, and, yes, they spend way too much time at the office, hockey arena, or Home Depot. Get over it.

Laundry, ironing, wiping the kitchen counter, emptying the dishwasher, sweeping the kitchen floor, making beds and grocery shopping *still suck*: These are not productive ways to spend our time, yet not only do we still engage in them, we sometimes consider the details of such activities worthy of conversation. They are not.

Children are awfully annoying a lot of the time: We know, we've heard it all before. They're annoying us now with the very things we did to annoy our own parents. What goes around, comes around. Snap out of it.

Tags: Annoying. Children. What else is new?

February 1
How BlackBerry Smartphones are like Toddlers

I've owned my toddler for a few years now (in fact, he's really like a re-tread since I've been through a few of them), but my tiny little baby Seamus is only a month old. It's been an interesting month—much like that adjustment to the first 4–6 weeks at home with a new baby, actually, only you're getting sleep and your boobs don't hurt. Or when that precious newborn infant transforms itself into a walking, talking, Tower of Toddler Terror. These life-changing events (childbirth, toddlerhood, and BB ownership) alter the way you view the world, and how you spend your time, and what's really important. In fact, there are quite a few similarities between new BB ownership and getting through life with a toddler.

1.   Mothers have been known to joke about how the only time they get to themselves is in the bathroom. Other mothers (especially those who own BBs) know this is a complete lie. The peaceful, private utopia usually lasts for only about 3.7 seconds, since both the toddler and the BB inevitably choose the most inopportune moment to interrupt with a whine, yell, thump, or buzz. They have impeccable timing.

2.   The childless and the BB-less are quite similar: Compared to their parenting and wired counterparts, they just don't get it. They look with disdain at those who have given their lives over to these demanding creatures and, at the same time, explain their status via fear and/or self-deprecation. For example:

"I'd be afraid to get one of those things. It would take up all of my time."

Or

"I can barely take care of myself."

3. You've answered all the questions, soothed all the fears, and have powered down everybody and everything for the night. *Not*. As soon as you slip into that blissful and necessary deep sleep, you will be awakened by the sound of whining. Clearly, you didn't quite shut everything off. This happens most frequently on the night before a very early flight, the biggest presentation of your career, or your one shot on national television. (In this circumstance, at least, the electronic toddler has one clear advantage: there have been no reported cases of a BB oozing out any liquids that require immediate cleanup.)

4. If they're quiet, you're constantly checking them to make sure everything is okay. If they're loud and interrupting, you just want them to shut up and go away. When they do, the cycle starts all over again.

5. You love them. You hate them. They drive you crazy when they're "on" and look adorable when they're sleeping. Nothing in your life is more frustrating or adorable. There's no reasonable explanation.

Tags: Love. Hate. The whole damn thing.

February 7
It's a "Report" Card. Report it!

This weekend I met a couple who, once they found out my profession, had a suggestion about an article for me to write. It's incredible, by the way, what people will tell you knowing, in fact, even *hoping*, that it might turn up in print (yes, I'm talking about *you*, that nice pair who shared with me their table at the overcrowded Starbucks in Blue Mountain— I really should come with a warning sign). Anyway, this nice couple said I should write about the dangers of showing your children your report card. To which I laughed and replied, "Hey, yes! Been there done that. I showed my 13-year-old son my Grade 8 report card the other day and he's still laughing about my D in Health. You're right," I agreed wholeheartedly, "always maintain that you had good grades in order to keep some parental superiority in the house." No, no, no, they replied, quite earnestly. I'd clearly misunderstood. What they meant was not showing the child his or her *own* report card. Wouldn't it be just a terrible thing for children to know exactly what they are accomplishing (or not) in life, when they have mom and dad around to handily interpret it for them? These parents simply told their 13-year-old daughter that if she was doing her best, that was all they could ask. Aha! I thought—she's failing! They must have seen a look of superiority cross my face, because they immediately, emphatically stated, "Oh, she gets all As, but she doesn't *need* to know that."

Excuse me, but why the hell not? What are they protecting her from? Are they worried she will know she is a success at school? What if she starts failing? How does she get re-motivated? Am I missing something? (I don't always wear a helmet and I walk into things with my head a lot, thanks to Seamus, so missing something is a distinct possibility.) This girl was also a competitive gymnast who missed quite a few regular classes to attend, get this, competitions. So, what? We don't need to feel that competitive edge intellectually, as in a grading system, but we do need it athletically? Or maybe the parents take her out of the gymnasium *before* her scores are posted. As long as she knows she's done her best, what does it matter?

Generally speaking, I'm not an idiot. I get it. There are many new and wonderful protective measures that we take with our children, and, as a result, they are living longer. No more bouncing around in the backseat of a station wagon or popping tar bubbles in the middle of a hot paved road. I get that. I also totally understand the relatively recent plethora of legislation about car seats, helmets for every "head-cracking" activity, and being cautious at playgrounds and other public places. Protecting our children physically in a reasonable manner makes sense. Totally sheltering them from every single slightly traumatic event in their life does not.

These days, we protect children from, gasp, losing. Hence, the "thanks for showing up trophies" kids are awarded for every sport in which they participate. Where is the thrill in actually coming first if every other player on every other team gets the same hardware? Where is the lesson in losing—to accept defeat gracefully (at least in public) or to make the thrill of winning that much more special? And lastly, as individual sports don't tend to hand out hardware to one and all (think swimming, dance, figure skating), it can be quite demeaning for a child who doesn't play team sports to see her siblings' overloaded trophy shelves. I know. I have three kids who play team sports, and one who does not. The team sport crew has hundreds of trophies. She has one. Does this make her feel like a loser? Oh my god, what should I do?

Brace yourselves, folks: We're not all team players, and we don't all deserve to win. I'd like to keep the portion of my registration fee that these organizations spend on trophies. I'll likely need it to pay for the therapy my kids will need to help them get over their feelings of inadequacy. Or maybe I can figure out a way to not let them know if they won or lost that last hockey game.

Tags: Idiot parents. Smart children. Who knew?

February 9
A Different but Still Uncomfortable Type of Wedgie

A word to the wise: I just heard this today (again). I don't want to hear it again, and I won't be responsible for the BB-sized bruise you end up with on your forehead if I do.

"You work from home, right? Can you pick my kids up from the bus stop?"

Arrgh! For many women (myself included) who work from home and run their own businesses, it is very hard to find a place with either the "real" working woman, or the "real" stay-at-home mom. Working women will ask, "Are you enjoying your time off?" while the stay-at-homes will wonder, "Don't suppose you'll be able to fit in the school bake sale?" We are the lost girls—the "work at homes" or the "wedgies," as I like to call us. We're wedged between home (and hence family) and work—and we're just barely squeezing into either world (never mind our low-slung jeans). My years spent in the corporate world render me unable to use the word "wedgie" without thinking about what the acronym might stand for. How about Women, Employed, Domestic, Glamorous, Intelligent Entrepreneurs. Or maybe it's more like Weirdly Entertained by Doing Gruntwork Internally and Externally. Something like that, anyway. The point is that we find ourselves with many of the pros and cons of both worlds.

Working At Home	At Home, With Kids
Pro Sense of accomplishment	No pressure to achieve
Con No recognition	"What have I done?"
Pro Own timetable	Schedule wide open
Con "Where did the day go?"	Everyone assuming schedule wide open
Pro No dress code	Sweats can be dressed up!
Con Out of style	Jeans or sweats, sweats or jeans?
Pro No lame corporate strategies	Set own road map and goals
Con What was the end goal?	Does a clean house count?

The wedgie's biggest dilemma is trying to earn some sort of respect or recognition from either the working moms or the stay-at-homes. The best way to do this is to appear fully engaged in the endeavours of both groups—which naturally you are not. What you are is trying frantically to reschedule meetings around the recently announced field trip, taking conference calls at the Walmart on your way to pick up a child who has recently been diagnosed with head lice at school. You don't have enough time (or inclination, frankly) to bake cookies for the class party, but you can get out for a reading program. You can't commit to a once-a-week Early Arrival phoning program, but you can almost get to the front row of the Spring Concert (I swear the people in the first two rows are sitting there right now, as I write this, waiting.) You would volunteer in the classroom, but you haven't found the time to get to the local police station to "get approved."

If your child is sick, you can get there within an hour, but if he simply "needs" something for show and tell or a forgotten pencil crayon, tough luck. You pick your children up for lunch only on "special occasions," which happen about once a month—but every time you do, you somehow manage to run into the school busybody who gives you that knowing smirk about what a great thing you're both doing by picking up your children to take them away from the pressures of a full school day. You take them to Burger King, by the way, because you haven't had time to order the groceries off the Internet.

You have business cards—because you work, dammit—but you feel a bit silly because your home address and suburban area-coded phone number are on the front, and you designed the cards yourself; they are not the result of a nine-month communications rebranding project. You just hope you've spelled everything correctly. You still refer to an office job as a "real" job.

All in all, however, working from home can help to build the illusion of "balance," if not for yourself then at least for your envious office-locked former colleagues, and for the women who, every once in a while, see you dressed to kill at the corner coffee shop. As you deal with constipated 4-year-olds, lice-ridden 7-year-olds, aching-new-braces 13-year-olds, and exam-stressed-out 15-year-olds—while trying to approve galleys, schedule interviews, and enter the hockey practice schedule into your exploding BB—you know one thing for sure: You are a woman who really "has it all." The question is, do you really want it?

Tags: Picking out a Wedgie.

February 14
Happy Valentine's Day

Love is in the air. Being electronically transmitted, in all likelihood.

For reasons I can't explain, PeeWee Herman and, in particular, his show, *PeeWee's Playhouse*, has always held great appeal for me. Fans of the show (back me up here!) know that if PeeWee had had a BB, he would have married it—just like he did with the bowl of cereal. I now share this devotion. Not with cereal, people, but with my darling Seamus. It provides me with comfort, entertainment, advice, news alerts, laughs, and, most importantly, companionship. I am never alone when my little square black friend is with me. Allow me to explain the push-me-pull-me addiction of BB love. "Push" as in always wanting to be sending someone, somewhere, an email about *exactly* what I'm doing at that moment, and "pull" as in I have to know immediately what's in that email that just vibrated into my world.

The phenomenon is fairly easy to understand: Receiving an incoming email message is akin to having a note passed to you in class from the cutest boy in school. You *have* to look at it. You *need* to look at it. The need is especially strong when you are in a situation where you *can't* look at it (because to do so would either be rude or downright dangerous). It takes a huge amount of willpower not to look at an incoming message, though you can always tell how many messages you have waiting for you by counting the number of buzzes. This is both intoxicating and annoying.

You can tell the depth of my devotion by the following typical attributes (which any true BB lover will have):

- The telltale thin red line on the right side of my stomach by my hip, caused by leaning over while wearing the holder and a too-short t-shirt or by making the amateur's mistake of putting the clip straight onto a waistband rather than a belt.
- The feeling of the "phantom" (or BraxBerry Hicks) vibrations, causing me to immediately look at a "no new email screen" and then feign reading in case others have witnessed my pathetic act.
- The stunned "hmmm?" response I offer when people are speaking to me and I'm simultaneously trying to read an email.
- The glazed look that automatically creeps across my face once the hummmm hummm of an incoming email is heard and the opportunity to read is denied due to circumstances beyond my control (toilet training a child, for instance).
- A renewed interest in prayer—prayer that once the sound of an incoming email is heard, the person you are speaking with will instantly be called away.

How did this happen? It's my own fault, really. After months of pestering my husband to "put the damn thing down and listen to me" (like putting an electronic device down is even possible for a male unless it's on fire, and never mind the "listening part"), I decided that if you can't beat them, join them. And from the minute that sleek black square became a part of my life, I knew we would be inseparable. I have a love/love relationship with Seamus. There. I've said it. Happy Valentine's Day!

Tags: **True Love. My funny Valentine.**

February 22
Get a Grip, People

It continues to astound me how violent a reaction the mere existence of a BB can elicit from some in the parenting world. Today I went on a field trip with my 4-year-old son, and of course I continued to send and receive messages through all of the boring bits (okay, mostly for the whole trip except when that kid really looked like he was going to throw up). It got a little scary: One of the dads threatened to rip it out of my hands. He's a firefighter and he doesn't have one? Don't they have "real" emergencies to deal with? And don't even get me started on the disdainful looks I received from the hockey moms as I clicked away. These women should know that I do this during soccer and hockey games as well—a habit that could lead to missing a goal, or, more importantly, the opportunity to catch up on some nasty gossip about the one mom who didn't make it to the game. Back off sister. You, too, Daddy-O.

Tags: Double dog dare ya.

February 24
No BBSP for You!

I just read a report about how a busy urban hospital is issuing BBs to critical care doctors. Apparently, this is the fastest way for the docs to find out from an attending nurse that a patient is in distress. I think this is a fabulous idea, though I'm a little concerned about the doctor waiting for or anticipating these emails when he or she is supposed to be sewing up my chest or pulling out that baby. How are they supposed to distinguish between a buzz that says "Room 116 STAT. Patient's heart stopped," and one that's merely offering "25% off at Business Depot?" For that matter, why would this particular group of professionals be any more immune to whittling away hours playing BrickBreaker than your average accountant or lawyer?

> "Yes, sorry, the doctor is running two hours behind schedule. Oh, and by the way, *you* can't have your handheld device on in the waiting room."

What's with that rule, anyway? I'm a little concerned about the quality of electronics in both hospitals and airplanes—and all these declarations that state I can't turn on a cellphone or a BB for "fear of interference" with the equipment. If my BB or cellphone is powerful and/or dangerous enough to cause death and disaster, surely they would confiscate it from me, wouldn't they? Seriously, folks, I can't be trusted to monitor myself! I once absent-mindedly turned my BB on in a plane. When I clued in to what I'd done, I immediately started hyperventilating, expecting a SWAT team of flight attendants to swoop down on me.

Typically, I expect investment bankers, lawyers, bank executives, brokers (basically any profession where being an asshole is an admirable personal quality) and their ilk to carry a BBSP, but like any electronic device, once the early adopters have absorbed the exorbitantly high prices for these new toys, the rest of us are free to join in the party at a much reduced rate. Working as a freelancer, I kid myself that I require a BB to "stay on top of my work," while carting children around to various sporting and academic events. Really, it's to keep me in the gossip loop with friends and neighbours, something I desperately miss now that my days of working corporately have come to an end and I don't get that fantastic colleague interaction. What is it that the doctors were missing in their overbooked days? The satisfaction that comes with playing BrickBreaker if they happen to lose a patient?

Tags: Doctors. Lawyers. Assholes. Redundant.

February 25
Or for You!

Should everybody carry a BlackBerry smartphone? I've been contemplating this and I'd like to suggest that some of the nasty women at my children's school don't require one (no, not the teachers silly, the other *mothers*). Their grapevine has worked consistently well for the past 200 years, and half the fun is getting the facts wrong. Imagine the chaos that would ensue if the gossip was accurate (and this will happen once the phenomenon known as "broken telephone" is eradicated through clear, texted information). The only thing we'd have to rely on for misunderstandings and conclusion jumping would be the tricky issue of "tone" in an email. And believe me, these women have "tone." But still, it wouldn't be half as much fun without the verbal innuendo and eyebrow raising that accompanies most truly great gossip among women with time on their hands (who, me?).

Gossiping housewives aside, I can think of other entire professions that don't require a BB either. Consider:

• The psychic: Um, don't they already know what people want to tell them? I *can* see that the BBSP would be a boon to the psychic world if said psychic is able to check messages from outside during a reading. (Can you say "accomplice"?) Listen for that telltale buzz the next time you're in with Madame Zorba.

• Stay-at-home moms: Seriously (see gossip discussion, above).

- Firefighters: Okay, maybe for real fires—but don't they have a big, loud bell? And besides, they shouldn't be reading jokes about "How to know if you were born in the '80s" anyway. Shouldn't they be brushing up on life-saving techniques and stuff like that?
- Mail carriers: This is purely for their own safety. If these men and women are anything like the typical user—and why wouldn't they be?—they would continually be walking into streetlights, small pets, and traffic as they try to check their messages. Ditto for UPS employees, FedEx truck drivers—or really anyone who drives around all day and wouldn't be able to resist it.
- Lifeguards: The person drowning isn't the one calling, so they don't need to know. And no, BBs aren't waterproof yet.

Really, there should be some internal memo in the RIM marketing department to ensure that these groups are not targeted. It's just wrong.

Tags: RIM. Pay attention.

February 26
Change Is Good

I attended a cocktail party last week in a somewhat corporate setting. First, it provided me with some reassurance that most of the people in the "real" world do indeed own BBSPs. Whew. It also offered a good opportunity to witness the changes that have taken place in that "real" world since I left it to journey to the dark side of "stay-at-home-momdom." I was introduced to a woman who explained her role at a large organization as that of a "change agent," or "helping others to manage change." Hmmm. I seem to remember rumblings about this at the monolithic organization where I used to work. Basically, these poor souls are meant to be the human buffers between senior management's new and exciting organizational strategies and the regular people who are just trying to earn a paycheque and keep the business operating. Surprisingly, those two things do go hand in hand, a fact often overlooked by the aforementioned strategically burdened senior management. A "change agent," by definition, is supposed to help those who are stuck to move forward—or at least in the direction that their company wants them to move in, which can be backward, but it's all about change. Embrace it.

It occurred to me that having a change agent on the home front could be a fabulous way to get my subordinates (i.e., my husband and children, and, if I'm lucky, even my neighbours and friends) to move things along in the way that I want things moved along. Otherwise known as the way nature intended.

For example:

- It used to be cute when my 2-year-old yelled "cowabunga" and ran at me before leaping into the air and landing on my lap, full force. Not so cute now that she is 8 and many pounds heavier (not to mention that my back isn't what it used to be). My kids need a "managing change" session on inertia versus impact and its accompanying results (do the words "time out" mean anything, Junior?)
- Being hungover was a minor inconvenience in my child-free, carefree younger days. These days, I need to learn how to manage the hangover-day expectations (beyond, of course, searching out greasy food, scarfing Tylenol and drinking Coke Slurpees). The session could be called "The Care and Feeding of Children—Even in the Face of Diversity" (i.e., a potential vomit situation—mine, not theirs).
- Video games are for pre-pubescent boys, not husbands. War games are for freaks who live in their parents' basements. Responsible adults don't need to waste time shooting fictional things with fictional weapons and feeling good about beating a high score. A change agent could transition your activities into something a little more productive—like battling those dust demons under the bed, or scraping off a crusty pan. (Author's note: playing BrickBreaker on one's BBSP is totally acceptable as it falls under the category of "finger and reflex exercises," which can be utilized in future fast-flying email conversations.)
- The neighbour's dog used to be cute, the way it jumped across our lawn and licked the children. Well, sort of. Now it's just an annoying, pooping sort of disturbance that we don't need. The 12-year-old doesn't want to play with your dog

anymore, neighbour. It's your dog, not mine. If I wanted one, I'd have one. Get a canine change agent to work on that, please.

Other smaller things that require change in my house right now include my son's underwear, the sheets on all of the beds, the central vac bag in the garage, the bathmat in the kids' bathroom, the baking soda in the refrigerator, my entire wardrobe, and the attitude of my teenage son. Maybe if I can think of all this as a strategic objective for the next fiscal operating period I can get some energy behind it. Or maybe I just need to "change" into my "going-out" jeans and find a martini bar.

Tags: Change. Good. All good.

February 28
Look Away, I Dare You, Just Look Away!

I'm an extrovert by nature, but the isolating nature of one-to-one email contact appeals to me in a way I can't quite describe. Ignoring the humming vibration of an incoming message is as hard as trying not to notice that first varicose vein that appears during your pregnancy. You don't want to obsess about it, but the more you try not to look at it, the more compelling it becomes.

It is relatively easy to pass judgment on us tuned-in, yet tuned-out creatures known as Blackberrians. We all did this with cellphone users, and it's likely the real Luddites looked down their noses at their friends who used black rotary telephones. Before you judge, however, try this: The next time you receive a personal letter or note, don't open it for at least two hours. It will give you a small sense of the desperate life that my emailing pals and I endure.

Tags: Judge this.

March 1
Guide to a Man's Domestic Duties

There are times when we inadvertently get a glimpse of someone else's life, and it can affect us in disturbing and thought-provoking ways. It happened to me tonight when I was at a book club meeting at a close friend's house. There he was, bold as brass, carrying on like it was a totally normal thing to do. Her husband. Walking right past us with a full laundry basket, going up the stairs, apparently to sort it and put it away.

I've had the occasional sighting of some of my male neighbours schlepping in the grocery bags. I have even encountered a few of them at the painful school concerts. As unproven studies would suggest, there are many men in today's modern world who do their fair share of work around the house, and with the kids. While this is a fabulous evolution from their caveman roots, what I haven't seen happening is the execution of some of the smaller chores they leave behind on a regular basis. Just yesterday I overheard a woman complain that her husband inexplicably left an empty cheese wrapper in the sink because he was "in a rush." Don't get it. These guys still have an expectation that "someone" will take care of all of life's little chores (which can take up to 12 hours a day to complete, if done correctly). I'm talking about things like:

- leaving the glasses on the counter for the dishwasher fairy,
- refilling the toilet paper supply in the bathrooms,
- leaving the sock lying languidly *next* to the laundry basket,

- walking right past the bathroom towels after mucky little fingers have had their way with them,
- not making their own doctor's appointments,
- not stopping on the way home from work to pick up paper towels or milk or bread or whatever.

Yes, this list is boring and endless. So are these chores. Yet somehow, women manage to own most of them. When we leave a glass on the counter, it's because we plan on coming back to it later, or because we didn't have time to put it away due to little Johnny's bleeding knee or Janie's full-facial-sneeze emergency. Yes, *we* really were in a rush. When *they* leave the glass on the counter, it's because . . . well, I don't know exactly why they do it, but they do it, and I find myself dutifully putting it away. So here's the question: Why *don't* they do it? And, for that matter, why *shouldn't* they?

In my next life, I want to come back as a man, if only to eliminate the ownership of some of these tedious and never-ending tasks. I want to be the one to say, "oh, really?" when my wife announces that we're out of toilet paper. I want to tell her to pick up some garbage bags the next time she's out, and to remember to call about that thing that's knocking around in the car. Is this too much to ask? Of course, with some forceful nagging and the withholding of favours, women can actually force men to get these jobs done, but how can we push responsibility across to the other side of the table once and for all?

One of the most annoying aspects of "sharing" responsibilities with a partner (who might be someone you would never, under any circumstances, choose to go into any sort of business with), is that he will likely have a different (i.e., wrong) way of doing things. And he may also pretend that he doesn't know what he's doing most of the time so that he doesn't have to do it anymore. He *is* pretending . . . right? He can't possibly still need instruction on how to use the washing machine, unload a dishwasher, make a bed, or go grocery shopping. Bloody hell, there are signs at the grocery store that tell you where to go and what to buy and how to pay. Yet apparently most men are still lost there. I suppose I should be more understanding, because I think if we examine this more closely, we'll discover that there are many, many male-specific barriers in place that prevent men from being effective and efficient in this particular setting. Consider:

• Asking a store clerk where the mangoes are is akin to *asking for directions*, which most men would never do. Furthermore, asking what a mango *is*, is just plain embarrassing. And why should he need to know? If he doesn't know what a mango is, we can't possibly need it for anything anyway. We were just being cute, right? Right?

• Men don't understand that the grocery list contains "must buy" items, but that there are also acceptable "impulse buys." In fact, some of these impulse buys could, in fact, be "should buys"—things that end up on the list thanks to a bit of initiative.

• Men need to clue into the fact that the point at which the checkout clerk asks, "Did you find everything you need?" is the *perfect* time to ask about those items they a) couldn't find, or b) didn't understand (see mango discussion above). Honestly, they shouldn't worry—chances are their wives didn't actually put any vagina-related products on the list. Unless she was being cute. In which case . . .

• The vagina-related products. Seriously. Get over yourself and buy a pack of tampons. They won't bleed all over your hands. Sheesh.

- All cereals, cookies, granola bars, and fruit chews are *not* the same. When we write down "Tropical Fruit Shrek 3 Chewy Buttons," we mean "Tropical Fruit Shrek 3 Chewy Buttons." Not the Citrus Fruit ones, not the Chewy Strings, and not the Jungle Book ones. Come home with any of these and you will be going back to the store. The store brand chewies purchased on sale will remain uneaten, unless you eat them yourself.
- If something like lobster, roast beef, caviar, or sparkling wine is on sale, buy it. Even it's not on the list. Go crazy. It's an impulse.

Women know men are confused a lot of the time. We know *we* confuse them. But the tactical jobs should be easy to execute. Finding the spot remover just shouldn't be as hard as finding, well, the G spot. Go to it, men. Some further tactical tips to help you through the day might include lessons on how to strategically plan the seating chart for the van before the children are throwing punches over the back row and you're already running 15 minutes late for the hockey game; why you should never throw out baby toys without burying them in the bottom of the garbage can (not sticking out of the top); not caring exactly why Junior has to have his left mitten on before his right mitten and just doing it; and understanding that saying, "I'll take care of dinner . . . so what shall I make?" is extremely irritating and not in the least bit helpful.

Domestic tasks are not willingly taken on by men. No shit. They're not willingly taken on by women either. Most of us hate them. But somehow, we always seem to own them. So ladies, find their hiding places, track them down, make them commit—go ahead and use all those skills that got them to marry you in the first place. It'll be worth it.

Tags: Men. Lists. Necessary.

March 5
Cheap Thrills Only a BlackBerry Smartphone Addict Can Get

As I discover the utility of the BB, I'm also discovering many benefits of ownership that are simply not covered in the *User's Manual*. Discovering these hidden and unexpected joys is not dissimilar to the realization that it is, in fact, quite different to actually be a parent than to read or hear about being a parent. If you are still without a BB, or a child, let me just share some of the moments you can look forward to:

The Blackberry smartphone:
- The glare of the boxy screen in your dark bedroom as you anxiously turn it on, even before fully opening your eyes. It's alive!
- Watching the email counter roar upward when you flip on the device. You are loved!
- The sight of a fully charged battery and a full telecommunications signal. All systems go.
- Being able to open the attachment.
- Catching your BB before it slides off your dangling belt and onto the manky washroom floor beneath your feet.
- Seeing someone else reading their emails at a solemn occasion (weddings, awards ceremony, annual review) and knowing it's okay to go for it.
- Finding yourself stuck in the waiting room at the doctor's, the gate at the airport, the hallway at your kid's school, or the

school bus stop and feeling those two insistent vibrations that tell you that a new world awaits.

• Receiving any email that doesn't have "Congratulations Lottery Winner," or "Staples Business Supplies Blowout Sale Special" in the subject line.

• Hitting "send" on a laborious email just seconds before being dragged into a meeting, sexual encounter, or long-awaited washroom stall.

• During an intensive session with "BrickBreaker," your ball seemingly shoots down through the bottom of the screen, only to reappear in the opposite top corner. Currently under review by the Catholic Church as a modern-day miracle.

• Hitting more than one "life" bubble on a single level of BrickBreaker.

• Thinking you've forgotten your cherished device at home on the hall table, only to discover it cheekily hidden beneath a glove in your purse.

The Child:

• Getting out of clearing up at huge family gatherings simply by waving a hand in front of your face and saying "Phew, I think this little one needs a change. I'll get to it right after I help carry away a few dishes and scrub some pots. The smell isn't bothering anyone, is it?"

• Making snide remarks about in-laws and half hoping/half dreading they'll come echoing out at the next family gathering, where you can trot out the line "Out of the mouths of babes, eh?"

• Taking advantage of free babysitting. "You really don't mind taking the twins for the entire afternoon? But I feel bad because you don't have any young kids to foist off on me . . ."

- Getting a note in your child's backpack that apologetically explains why the "Math Can Be Fun!" fundraising night has been cancelled due to an unexpected leak in the school sprinkler system.
- Picking up a voice message that says "Due to severe thundershowers, tonight's soccer game is cancelled. No makeup game has been scheduled."

Are you sensing a theme here? A lot of cheap parental thrills come from the cancellation of previously scheduled kid-oriented/parent-guilt-driven events. For example, these classics:

- "Thanks for offering to come on the Grade 1 field trip, Ms. Buckworth, but we already have enough volunteers to help us out on our Sports & Cheese Museum Tour."
- We regret to inform you that all of our volunteer coaching positions have been filled for this year's soccer season. (This is pure fantasy. Such a thing has never happened in the history of children's amateur sport.)
- "If you don't mind, Kathy, I'll just add your raffle ticket books to mine. I know I can unload them at my next family reunion. It's no trouble, really. Your kids can even share the 'most tickets sold' award."
- Due to a shortage of gold plastic, trophies will not be given to every single player at this tournament, only to the winning team.
- Kindergarten Graduation Night has been cancelled. Because it's stupid and we've finally recognized that.

Don't get me wrong, parenting is not *all* fun and games

and cheap thrills, as much as this list might suggest. There truly are some moments of terror that come with owning and mastering these little slices of heaven. Tune in tomorrow—if you dare. *Mwha ha ha ha ha ha.*

Tags: Thrills. Cheap and even cheaper.

March 6
Stop! You're Scaring Me!

You came back! Good for you. Owning a child or a BBSP is definitely not for the nervous or meek. Settle in and prepare yourself for the horrifying incidents you'll inevitably face with both:

The BB:
- Seeing the "red" battery light when you are miles away from the closest recharger and computer.
- Accidentally hitting delete on an unread email. You're sure it was *the* one.
- Getting your elbow knocked on a previously undiscovered (to you) level of BrickBreaker. By your 6-month-old, whom you can't *really* yell at—or teach to not do it again.
- Turning it on and finding no new messages. Loser.
- Driving, with your children, on the way to something important (no, really important, like the emergency room, not a hockey game) and not being able to make a single move toward releasing your heavily buzzing BB and placing it on the seat beside you.
- Going for a once-yearly manicure and listening to the buzzing from inside your purse for a whole hour. Who needs perfect nails? Go for it! (This is similar to hearing the buzzing while "relaxing" during the first five minutes of an hour-long massage. Who can relax now?)
- Giving your spouse grief for checking his email in the

middle of dinner, just because *you* don't have any new messages. Once the guilt trip is launched, your own BlackBerry goes off. Excuse me, ladies' room?

• "Letting" your 3-year-old try BrickBreaker for the first time. Okay, that's enough.

• Facing the people you made fun of when they had a BB and you didn't.

• Being on level 13 of BrickBreaker with only 2 lives left. You had only one life "bubble" go by, for god's sake.

• Having your spouse pick up your BB to send a quick note as you simultaneously realize that the one slightly flirtatious note from a member of the opposite sex you've received in the past 17 years is still sitting in your inbox.

Can these be matched by horrifying moments of parenting? You bet your BB.

If you're a parent, you know that moments of "sheer terror"—or at least thoughts of "I am so screwing up another human being"—take up most of the minutes in a normal parenting day. Are my kids smart enough? Did they drink enough milk today? Hey, that kid down the street is six months younger and he's a reader! When I call my teenage daughter a loser, she knows I'm kidding, right? What about when I tell the 14-year-old to run away and see if I care. Does that spot near his eye require a doctor's appointment or can I pretend I didn't notice it? If he pulls the wings off a fly, is he headed for mass murder? If I don't buy her a dog, will she never learn responsibility? If I do buy her a dog, and I end up taking on all of the responsibility, have I taught her that Mommy will forever clean up her mess? Why does he have to run through a parking lot? Why do they think it's funny to talk about when they're dead one day? Do I really want my 4-year-old son to French kiss me? It's totally normal for a 14-year-old boy to have absolutely no redeeming qualities, right?

Have I scared you yet? Good. My teenage daughter just walked in the door with the *New Drivers' Manual*, so I needed to pass some of it on.

Tags: Terror has a new name.

March 8
Step Away from the BB.
Okay, That's Far Enough.

Moderation in the use of a BBSP can be a good, and, um, moderating thing. The same can be true in parenting. I don't really want to spend all of my free time with either Seamus or my other children. Really. I need a life. As a parent, I always remind myself that an additional benefit of having the children out of my presence for considerable amounts of time (anywhere from half a day to a month away at summer camp) is that it makes it easier to blame any socially unacceptable habits on caregivers. Be warned: if they are in your care 24/7, the blame rests solely with you (don't even try to use the TV/electronic gaming influence—*you* provide that entertainment, after all). I personally love the "running with the wrong crowd" excuse that parents of teenagers trot out. Has there ever been a parent in the history of parenting who was willing to admit that his or her child was the one leading the others astray? Where do *these* kids come from?

But I digress. Having my BB become inoperable and having my children out of sight have much in common. While I enjoy the reprieve from the constant attention-seeking little devils, at the same time, I'm more than a little anxious to have them reappear and reaffirm that my time on earth is both recognized and meaningful.

Tags: Turn. It. Off.

March 18
This Is Progress?

In this age of Modern Parenting, everything is more complicated, overscheduled, and overanalyzed. Welcome to the world of "Playdates," which have silently and stealthily replaced the simplicity of "Can Jennifer come out and play?" As children, we used to (gasp) organize ourselves! Without a walkie-talkie, cellphone, or hovering mother at the end of the driveway! Although I'm not sure how this happened, I recently found myself watching a parenting television show in which the hosts "explained" how I, too, could pull off the most perfect of all playdates. One of the hosts honestly expressed that she didn't even know what the term meant (I love this woman!). Once defined for her, she replied, "Oh, you mean like a kid comes over to my house to play?" *Yes!* *Yes!* I silently screamed from my couch position, but *no*, apparently! At least according to the other overzealous host. Just watch this clip and you'll see, she said.

Well, the staged video clip had her preparing the living room, moving in all of the toys, costumes, and other paraphernalia her 5-year-old might want to pull out with friends. She then went to the kitchen, where she laid out a special kiddie plastic tablecloth, matching plates, special kiddie treats! The works. She also prepared Mommy treats for the Mommies (and, frankly, none of it looked like wine) and settled in to entertain *them* for a couple of hours as well. Huh? Tell me this doesn't happen in real life! Isn't the real purpose of having your kid go out to play so you can have a couple of hours unfettered by children, child-like things, and their appendages (i.e., mothers)? What happened to throwing the offspring in the basement with some mismatched Lego and a half-eaten bag of chips? I used to be even more cavalier than that, before the unfortunate incident that involved an overprotective mom's child running upstairs with my husband's camping axe. Why do "those" kids always find these things? Note to self: If engaged in '50s-style "playdates" (i.e. the unsupervised, unstructured, kids-only type), make an effort to sweep the basement at least once a month.

What a perfect example of how Modern Mothers have elevated even the most simple of things—"Can Johnny come out and play?"—to "How is Dakota's schedule for next week?" The mom/host/freak on the television parenting show even admitted that her daughter had her own scheduler to keep track of her lessons, social engagements, etc. At 5. Maybe I'm being a bit unfair to her (I have been a guest on this show and I found the ladies to be quite fun), but this type of show is obviously geared to "today's new mom." Where is it written that the "new mom's" mandate is to complicate everything, and make regular (i.e., nervous) moms feel totally inadequate when they find themselves pulling out that half-eaten bag of chips and struggling to remember the visiting kid's name (I use "axe-boy" over here now). This is a trend I can definitely do without. As should all Modern Mothers. And luckily, it's easy enough to avoid. Just turn on your BB and say you're too busy.

Tags: Playdates. Descent into hell.

March 25
Places Where Children and BBSPs
Are (Gasp!) Not Welcome

As hard as it is for parents and BerryHeads to believe, there are some situations in which it is not at all appropriate to have either children or the beloved BB in active service. As the self-defined Mother of All Users, I am happy to share helpful tips for Modern Mothers who haven't yet faced such dire straits. Learn from my experiences. Please.

Places not to use your BB:
- While watching your child's monologue in the Grade 2 class play! Particularly if you are playing BrickBreaker with the volume on high.
- While in bed during more, er, intimate moments.
- When you are in the middle of a conversation with someone and you are supposed to be "listening" (i.e., not talking or doing something else).
- While you are driving—except at red lights. Pre-train a child in your care to yell "yellow light, Mom" when the change is a comin'.
- While bathing a small child. Oh, you're right there so the kid will probably be fine, but you might get your fine instrument wet and not be able to use it for a few hours.
- While swimming—see above.
- Just after eating an entire bag of cheesies—the keys will never be the same.

- During any type of surgical operation—your spelling will be atrocious and blood is as bad as water for damaging the internal organs (Seamus's, not yours. Seriously.)
- At fondue parties—hot oil, angry spouse, ignored friends—need I say more?
- While attending funerals, memorial services, weddings, or other "more important" and supposedly serious events. Like, besides the dead guy, you're telling me the other guests and participants aren't dying to see what that vibrating was about too?

You will likely also come across some real psychos who will tell you not to look at your BB while in school playgrounds. Come on! Talking to other parents is boring, and you'll probably be willing to risk that dodgeball to the head just to get to that company gossip. The true user epitomizes the "grass is always greener" mentality. It's not unlike the urge that grips store clerks who answer the phone instead of serving you, the person standing right in front of them.

This peeking over the fence at the "havemores" (i.e., those of us who have BBs) also affects many people who wish they had children as wonderful as yours—well, mine, actually. People who have children are always thrilled to see other children acting up (because they have *so* been there), while people who don't have children are shocked and dismayed at the parents' lack of parenting skills. There are some people who welcome children, all children, but these people are very hard to find. And, let's face it, there are some places where it is totally inappropriate to bring the little angels—no matter how well behaved. (Truthfully, I seek these places out and then add them to my own list of "wish I could take you sweetie, but..."

destinations. Then I inch my way out of the front door alone.) You might want to tack these to your own fridge.

It is ill advised to take children to:

• The "naughty" store, local pub, strip joint, or an X-rated movie, except in extreme emergencies. First off, only two of them serve drinks. And the other two could result in having to either take your husband with you, or do an in-house demo upon your return. Choose and use wisely.

• Friends' houses for dinner, especially when where you know the likely outcome is going to be your child choking that annoying smartypants of theirs; a bodily function mishap you can't explain after the age of 7; or the predictable turn of events when you discover that your "friends" are actually weirdos who don't believe in using technology as a babysitter. Family Monopoly, anyone?

• Relatives' homes that are deliberately not childproofed since "children have to learn what not to touch." Items on display could include a 712-piece collection of highly breakable and ridiculously expensive glass figurines, and an unopened toy collection from the '50s.

There is a fortune to be made by some entrepreneurial sign maker who invents a reversible No Admittance sign with the word "Children" on one side and "BBs" on the other. Noncompliers to be punished by the full force of the law.

Tags: Forbidden. Signs.

March 27
Okay. Okay. You Guys Win.

This morning my husband stood in front of me in the kitchen, spread his arms wide open and said "Okay, it's Saturday. We have nothing on. Tell me what you need me to do today." Man, that pissed me off. Yes, I know he thought he was being a good guy and yes, many women might love to hear these words. But it all comes down to this for me: Why do *I* have to be the one to tell *him* what to do in this house? Why do I own it? I want to live like they do, I really do.

I actually think about this a lot, and so, some thoughts on why it really is better to be a man than a woman:

- No one expects men to wear thong underwear. In fact, why is it that they don't get a visible panty line even when wearing briefs? I don't get it.
- Men only have to shave their face. Or backs if they have a wife who can see. Or feel. Ewww.
- No PMS, monthly period, hot flashes, leaking breasts, Pap smears, et cetera, et cetera. Maybe a bit of jock itch. Please. Amateur stuff.
- Men are completely, blissfully unaware of the many, many slights that can be dished out at bus stops, school concerts, or in grocery store lineups. Women are aware of all these nuances. Too aware.
- Men literally can have nothing on their minds, except a naked lady. How freeing is that?

- Men honestly don't care if they can't find a single Tupperware lid in the house.
- Men don't worry about "shopping off the list" at the grocery store. They just never do it. If it isn't on the list (which their wives wrote for them), they obviously don't need it. Easy peasy.
- Watching professional sports can be considered a hobby. Knowledge of statistical facts surrounding these sports can be misinterpreted as "knowing something" by other men.
- Grey hair. When women get it, we instantly look 10 years older. When men get it, even the most disgusting slovenly pig is suddenly considered "sophisticated."
- If men are losing their hair, they can simply shave their heads. Unless auditioning for the remake of *The Coneheads*, this is not so much an option for women.
- Men's children get their last name automatically (versus having to make a big case for it and having your husband be called "whipped" and you being called a "ballbreaker") even if yours is a far, far, superior surname.
- Men can use the phrase "I'm sorry, I just wasn't thinking." And people believe them. Because it's true.
- Even if men wear socks with sandals, they can still potentially pick up a chick. Trust me.
- Bikini waxing. Enough said.
- Men really don't care if the sheets ever get changed. Ask them to guess how often this should happen. Ballpark it! Wrong!
- Yes, it *is* very important what that cow down the street said about your teenaged daughter.
- Men can be completely unencumbered by petty details. The fact that garbage day has been on the same day of the week

for 17 years makes no difference; they still need to be reminded to take it out.

- Men can find endless hours of entertainment at Canadian Tire, Home Depot, or Mark's Work Wearhouse. What is that about? Don't you like shopping in real stores at a civilized mall?
- Men don't question the nutritional value or hygienic pedigree of any type of fast food. Not hotdogs at the ballpark, French fries from the chip truck, the Salisbury steak from the Zeller's diner, or even the cheese on the chili cheese dog at the beach hut. Bliss.
- If a man forgets to phone a friend back, or invite him to a get-together, he didn't do it on purpose. He actually simply forgot. And the friend isn't mad. He could not care less. Sweet.

Despite these many advantages, men did end up having their sex organs placed on the outside, which admittedly leaves them vulnerable to the groin shots we shriek hysterically at on *America's Funniest Videos*. Feeling sorry for yourselves? Reminder: We do childbirth. Just take what you can and be thankful you're not a hermaphrodite. And you know what you can do for me today? Change those frigging sheets.

Tags: Unfair. Unreasonable. Pass the wine.

April 2
Neither a Lender Nor a Borrower Be

Some people can't bear to have their children out of their sight for more than a few minutes. It makes them frantic. I, on the other hand, have the opposite reaction: There's nothing I like more than when a friend (or even passing acquaintance) offers to take my young children off my hands for a few hours. Like today. For a few giddy hours, after the nice new neighbour lady had taken them away, I ran around thinking "what can I do while the kids aren't here?" (Turns out my imagination needs some boosting, but my closet has never been tidier.)

There is a downside, however. Your children may reveal some unsavoury habits to your new best friend, and, worst of all, you'll be expected to take on her kids once in a while.

I'm a little bit embarrassed to admit that while I'll send my kids off with almost anyone, I don't have these same slack regulations about letting Seamus out of my sight, or, more frighteningly, touch. Similarly, I have learned that there is quite a long list of reasons that I don't want to borrow someone else's.

The Top 10 Reasons Not to Borrow a BlackBerry smartphone:
1. First of all, what, you don't have your own? You are broadcasting your loser status to the entire world!
2. If you do have one that is temporarily indisposed (breathe, breathe), the one you borrow will inevitably be slightly different. This will lead to either feelings of inadequacy ("you can

download tunes on yours?") or superiority ("I'm not used to this original version"), both of which are bad Berry karma.

3. The owner might have last employed the device while in the bathroom.

4. The owner might be a nose picker. Or worse.

5. If you borrow someone's BB and the keys are sticky, what are you going to do? Give it back without sending a message? You're trapped. Gross.

6. You might inadvertently look at the owner's BrickBreaker score and decide that they're either a loser (they have a higher score than you) or that they're a loser (they have a lower score than you). You can't win.

7. Malaria, West Nile Virus, the common cold, the bird flu (hey, wasn't she just in China with that thing?).

8. You discover the owner's battery is dead and that he's just been pretending to be cool. You can't be friends with him anymore.

9. She has more unread messages in her inbox than you do. She wins.

10. Back to #3: He certainly *took* it to the bathroom. How much do you want to bet he used it before washing his hands?

Similarly, handing my precious Seamus off to a virtual stranger (actually, the stranger is not virtual. He's standing right in front of me, and he's about to be very real on my BlackBerry) can be a terrifying experience. Did I erase those notes? Does he know what he's doing? Does he have a steel plate in his head that will cause me to lose my entire address book, or worse, my BrickBreaker score?

The Top 10 Reasons Not to Lend a BlackBerry smartphone:

1. The potential lendee has disdained you for carrying it and looking at messages all the time, and now he wants to send a note to his wife about the train being delayed for two hours the night of his child's first school concert? I don't think so.

2. She'll see my BrickBreaker score.

3. He'll see my empty inbox.

4. She might wander off to the bathroom with it.

5. As with the borrowing dilemma, I don't know where his hands have been, and now they're going to be all over my little keyboard and spinning wheel. I can't Windex my BB, people!

6. A message could come in while she's using it and it might be a message I don't want shared (e.g., From: Dr. Smith/Subject: Prescription for Oozing-Rash Cream).

7. A message *doesn't* come in while he's using it, and he's had it for more than two minutes. Nobody loves me.

8. She could send a dirty message to everyone on your distribution list. She's a geek, after all (remember she doesn't have a BB of her own? Hello!).

9. It's hard to read what he's typing from over his shoulder unless you get the screen lined up just so.

10. Why are you friends with these people, anyway? And, oh great, what's that Band-Aid all about? And on the "wheeling" finger, no less.

The bottom line is this: children and BBSPs are all about ownership, one upmanship and petty jealousies. That's why they're a perfect marriage for today's Modern Mom. After all, it's how a lot of us "parent" today. And by the way, did you notice that when "parent" transformed from a noun to a verb it became much more serious and competitive? Like we needed that!

Tags: Don't. Even. Ask.

April 7
Let It Go . . .

I've revised my thinking on lending out children. Rather, I've revised the criteria I have for the recipients. You already know I don't want to "borrow" someone else's children. This is self-explanatory to anyone who has been sucked into the charming and joyous sounding "playdate," as we've already discussed. There is nothing remotely playful or date-able about a playdate. A playdate basically involves having unpaid responsibility for someone else's child, who will likely teach your child one thing you wish he/she didn't know (i.e., how to do backflips off the couch, interesting new terminology for private body parts, that sort of thing). Alternatively, your little guest might spend his or her time at your house gathering intelligence to take back over enemy lines (to you-know-who down the street). This will cause you either to have to act in a civilized manner with your own children and be extra nice to them, or to let the mini-guests gather away and suffer the consequences yourself. (Note to self: There is a definite upside to being banned from the Parent Council.) I now only, only, take on someone else's child if I know that said child will keep my own child(ren) entertained in a separate room in the house.

Having my children go to someone *else's* house for a play-date can also be problematic. Yes, it's lovely to have them out of the house at *that* unpaid babysitter. At the same time, though, I have to remember that my child will be unsupervised by me and is likely to swear, spit, punch, backflip, tell tales, be rude—you know, have normal childhood behaviour without me there to say "I don't know where that came from! That's a new one!"

Here's my big revelation: The best people to "lend" your children to are, ironically, the childless. Grandparents and other relatives whose children have grown have unrealistic expectations. Time can do wonderful things with the memory, causing these kind folk to forcibly blank out any childhood behavioural issues or bad parenting episodes from their pasts. No, I'm talking about the truly childless here. These men and women don't have any expected norms. It is so great to hear single aunts and uncles wail after a weekend with their nephews and nieces, "Wow, those kids really wore me out! I don't know how you do it full time." At the same time, you'll get all kinds of praise for your stamina and patience. The childless rarely say, "Those kids were little buggers and I'm sure it wasn't *my* lack of parenting skills causing the problems." Lending my children out to just the right people can be beneficial for my sanity, but lending to the "wrong" people (those who actually know what constitutes good behaviour for a 4-year-old, or when a child should truly be potty trained or soother-free) can cause more harm than good.

Tags: Take my kids, please.

April 15
When They're Good, They're Very, Very Good

I expected Seamus to make my life a little simpler and a little more organized, and, of course, to improve my "coolness" ratio. I'm also discovering that it can deliver little pieces of heaven anytime, anywhere. Nice! For instance, I just got the following email from my best friend:

> "Want to meet for cocktails tonight? Lori [her teenage daughter] is on her way over to sit for you."

I immediately emailed her back, thanking her for the little piece of heaven and sharing my thoughts on this added bonus of BBSP ownership. To illustrate my point, I told her about some other nice bits of news that had reached me in this way. For example:

- "We sold your book rights to China! (P.S., there are lots of people there, in case you didn't know)."
- "Passed you on the street today but didn't recognize you as I thought your ass was much wider than that! Magic pants or a slimmer you?"
- "Saw your son helping out a friend at the schoolyard today—he must have wonderful parents!"
- "You've been invited. . . ." Actually, it doesn't matter to what. It's being invited that counts, not whether you want to, or can, go.

- "We like your article and want to commission you to write 10 more just like it! And our freelance rates have just gone up!"
- "Mom, can I sleep over at Janna's for her 16th birthday tonight? I know you're having some people over for dinner and normally you'd love for me to hang around and make appropriate conversation, but maybe just this once . . . ?"
- "The Holiday concert has been cancelled due to an internal conflict on the school council. No makeup date has been set."
- "Hockey practice this week has been moved from 6:00 a.m. to 9:00 a.m. Sorry for any inconvenience this may cause."
- "The upcoming Professional Development Day has been cancelled (due to lack of teacher sign-up for the 'Motivate Yourself to Work Harder' seminar)."
- "This is Phoebe from Jenny Craig. Just a quick note to let you know our scale has been off by seven pounds (heavier) and we just noticed it! You're actually three pounds under your goal weight! Congratulations!"

I would be remiss, of course, if I didn't mention the flip side of this coin. A trusty BB can deliver notes that, judging by the subject line, are too frightening to open. I think that the world at large has clued in to this fact, because some senders will actually disguise the subject line just to reel me in, and whammo, I'm hooked. This is especially dangerous when the sender requests a receipt notification and I stupidly respond "yes." Some examples:

- Subject: Your son Alex is outstanding. . . .
in the hallway due to his apparent inability to refrain from drawing with red ink on his deskmate's arms.

- Subject: Your book sales are up . . .
stairs in the bins marked "out of print" and "one-hit wonders."
- Subject: Oprah wants to see you . . .
Oh, did I type Oprah? I meant Opera—the season starts today!
Don't forget to buy your tickets!
- Subject: Are you busy tonight?
Because we could really use a babysitter for the triplets and I
know you don't have much of a social life.
- Subject: I'll be on time for dinner tonight . . .
if you're serving dinner at midnight and you don't mind me
reeking of free holiday booze and garlic shrimp.
- Subject: Congratulations—you have won . . .
(I don't need to finish this one. You didn't really open this
email, did you?)

Some of the best notes I receive are from my children, but
they can also be the worst ones, too. The teenagers in my house
who communicate with me in this way often do so only to
avoid the dreaded "face time." Email is a handy way to get bad
news across without worrying about ducking or diving at the
same time. It's easier to type in "Mom, I have detention" and
then sign off quickly than to call from the school office. Apparently, voice time can be scary, too.

Tags: Notes. Heaven.

April 21
Whackjob? Oh, yes.

I just had a call from a radio producer responding to the pro-
posed comedy pitch a partner and I submitted months ago.
How exciting! How glamorous! How career enhancing! How...
bloody inconvenient.

The producer called my BBSP from Edmonton—halfway
across the country—at the precise moment that lovely 4-year-
old Nicholas started a meltdown in front of a $20 SpongeBob
wastebasket that I was refusing to buy him at Walmart. While
I transitioned from silently turning red-faced and making the
violent hand gestures universally accepted as meaning "No!"
to waving the item into the shopping cart, I can only hope I
gave the hapless producer an appropriate response to his question of why we think "Mommy Is a Whackjob" might be a
show to which other mothers could relate. I'm still waiting to
hear back. Perhaps he caught the anxiety in my voice and decided I couldn't deliver the dulcet tones much admired by our
national radio broadcaster. And yes, that wastebasket looks
great in Nicholas's room. Thanks for asking.

Tags: CBC. Call me.

May 2
A Real "Professional"

Now that I've grown somewhat accustomed to the addition of Seamus to my brood (five months of near constant use will do that to you), I find I'm best able to utilize the email function while:

- in cold hockey arenas,
- in the hallway waiting for a tutoring session to end,
- outside a principal's office (granted, the messages sent from that particular locale can be a little tense),
- in line at grocery stores,
- in children's dance studios,
- in the middle of a boring land-line phone conversation.
- having a pedicure, blow dry, or dye job (yes, that's blow dry and dye job, not what you thought. Emailing during sex is where one has to draw the line—and honestly, how much could you say in 30 seconds even if both of your thumbs were free?).

Yes, I know the constant emailing can seem pretentious and aloof, and no, I don't care. There is no one here to whom I actually want to talk. My buddies, on the other hand, never let me down.

It's all good in the land of the BB Mom. Or at least I can make it seem that way when I'm communicating only with this silent, toneless, anxiety-free textual device.

Tags: Blow. Job. Tricked ya again.

May 5
And in my spare time . . . I still have a life, right?

Today, my teenage daughter asked me if I could "drop by" the dance store (some 20 minutes away) to pick up some toe thongs for her, prior to her next class (i.e., tonight at 5 p.m.). Because, as she so eloquently put it, "It's not like you're doing anything else—except playing with Seamus."

One thing Modern Mothers rarely have is "spare time." The very word "spare" implies an excess of the item in question. Link it with the word "time" and you might just have the world's best example of an oxymoron. Only bored children truly have time to spare—which, while your back is turned, they will fill with activities such as scrubbing the bathroom sink with toothpaste, taking every single piece of Lego you own (approximately 997, by the way) and flinging them about the basement, or simply drawing a long black line (with the one permanent marker in your house) on your new red leather sectional sofa.

For women, and for moms, there is no such thing as free time. If a previously unscheduled moment should unexpectedly arise, there is always some fun-filled activity to slot in—an extra load of laundry, shuffling through the papers on the home-office desk, recovering a chair, sending emails, or emptying the dishwasher. (Okay, I threw in the wild and crazy chair recovering suggestion to see how many of you were paying attention. Please.) So, when the weekend comes (you know, that time of the week when children and husbands celebrate the fact that they're not at school or work, and when wives and moms start counting the seconds until they can get the buggers out of the house and get on with their own work or home lives), deciding how to spend "leisure" time can be quite a challenge. Grocery shopping? Laundry? Mopping the kitchen floor? Oh, and don't worry about asking your husband what to tackle first on that bright and sunny Saturday morning. You'll just catch a glimpse of his back as he scurries out the door to a) Home Depot, b) ski, c) nip into the office, or d) launch a crafty ruse that begins with him mumbling something about mowing the lawn or shovelling the driveway, but turns into a gabfest with a fellow escapee. And the children will either be moaning about how bored they are (while avoiding their own messy rooms and the pile of homework in the front hallway) or be suspiciously quiet apart from the little footsteps heard running across the floor overhead, punctuated only with "oops" or "that's okay."

Activities I need to get to (taking precedence over the frigging dance store) but haven't quite found the "spare time" to tackle, include:

• Going through my closet and drawers to pull out every piece of clothing I haven't worn in the past seven years. They will never fit, and yes, sometimes the no-underwear option is better than that raggedy pair, or the ambitious thong.
• Sorting out the linen closet so that the risk of an avalanche is diminished every time the door must be opened to stuff in yet another tiny washcloth.
• Cleaning the front hall closet, otherwise known as "the mitten widow-maker." You can find only baseball hats in the

winter and toques in the summer, alongside the 14 right-handed mittens. Just keep kicking in the stuff at the bottom until your husband freaks, does a massive cleanout, and moves everyone's coats, shoes, and boots to the other scary closet in the basement. Except for his own stuff, which he organizes quite neatly before heaving a satisfied sigh.

Tags: Spare Time. Mythology.

May 6
A Slight Correction

Okay, I confess. Last night I did find some spare time (don't tell my daughter). And I spent it drinking wine. So sue me. I'll admit that the demands of being a Modern Mother can often drive me to have, well, let's say, more than the *Canada Food Guide* might suggest in the category of veggies and fruits (there are grapes in wine, silly!). The semi-weekly "drink cart" (a throwback to the old days in advertising when the drink cart came wheeling by on a Friday afternoon . . . sigh) in our neighbourhood was again the culprit in a drinking-fest that found me regretting my actions this morning.

I have discovered, through my own painful personal experiences, that there are many, many circumstances in which a parent does *not* want to find themselves hungover. You think hangovers are bad when you're in college, or even as a young working married or single? Try throwing in the daily routines of a Modern Mother and you will long for the days when you could lie on the couch—greasy hamburger in one hand, ice-cold Coke in the other—and pray that your head would actually just either roll off or explode. Suck it up, princess. You just don't have the (spare) time to do this anymore. I'm off to the dance store. Wish me luck.

Tags: Head explosions. Whine. Wine.

May 13
Accessories Every BlackBerry User and Parent Needs

I just watched a segment on CBC's *This Hour Has 22 Minutes* that featured the BlackBerry smartphone Helmet and warning flag, designed to stop users from walking into light poles, buildings, et cetera, and to warn oncoming pedestrians of the users' presence. This was a very funny piece—mostly because it is true. There's not one hard-core BB user who hasn't walked into or off something they didn't see because they had their head down, thumbs a flying, wheel a spinnin'. That helmet and flag could definitely have a real-life application. And that got me thinking. There are quite a few other BBSP accessories I could use:

• *Fitted blazers/blouses/tops:* When women strap on BlackBerrys, it's often onto a belt or waistband. If you're wearing a fitted top, the awkward bump can add inches to either the waist itself, or, depending on the position, the stomach or thigh—all areas where most of us don't want to add anything. I have seen some women wearing them on the back of their pants, but frankly this looks weird and it's not very convenient . . . although it could provide a nice little lower back massage if the vibration were strong enough. I propose that clothing manufacturers design jackets with a small "pouch" that clearly shows that the wearer is in fact sporting a BBSP at her waist. This will avoid confusion with the results of that extra cheese plate you had last week. (If I have to post a "BB on Board" plastic sign on my back to avoid having someone think I've gained another few inches, so be it.)

• *Gunslinger/holster:* In the absence of the aforementioned pouch jacket, how cool would it be to have the BB "holstered" in an over-the-shoulder leather holder (Prada, Gucci, are you listening?) that the user could whip out before starting to tap away. Very cosmo.

• *Car magnifier:* There is nothing more frustrating to me than those times when I know I have a message but I just can't get to it—the best example being when I'm driving. I can look at maps, talk to friends, change the radio, pass food, put on makeup, but I just know I shouldn't pull it out when I'm zipping down the highway, or even stopped in traffic, for that matter. A device that mounts on the dashboard and magnifies the screen so that messages can be read while driving would be ideal. Even better if the sentences come up teleprompter style so that I don't lose my place while madly braking to avoid smashing into the car ahead.

• *Waterproof cover:* A natural. When I'm in the shower, or the bath, or the pool, or even in a rainstorm, it would be good to be able to whip on the waterproof cover and keep in touch. It's a 24/7 world, baby.

• *Abandonment alarm:* I'm in the car, I don't have a car magnifier (yet), so I pull out my BB and place it in the cupholder. I park, get out of my car, walk 3 kilometres through freezing snow, sit down in a comfy Starbucks, reach down to pull out Seamus for some one-on-one time and . . . it's not there. It's still in the cupholder, isn't it? Or, I'm on the commuter train platform. The train is late. No worries, I'll just stand here and look at my—oh damn, it's in the car, parked at the back of the lot, and here comes that frigging train. What we need here is a homing device/pager that emits a shrill shriek if the owner and the BB are separated by more than three feet. That's all it takes.

- *Belt Stopper:* I'm wearing a belt. Seamus is, of course, strapped to it. I go to the bathroom, in a public washroom, with a suspicious looking hard slate floor—wet, of course. I undo my belt, slide down my pants, do my thing (and yes, maybe even check a few emails), before placing it back in its holder to "finish up." I stand up, my belt points downwards and my entire BB device/holder unit slides off my belt right into a puddle on the hard floor. I get splashed, my pants are down around my ankles, and my BlackBerry shoots into the next stall. I need a clip, people, or some superglue, to keep this from happening. I will always email in the bathroom—I just need some help.

Tags: Prada. Gucci. Patent Pending.

May 14
Accessorize This, You Little Rats

Yesterday's post really got me thinking about the whole accessory thing. Okay, I'll admit it. Couldn't sleep last night just thinking of ways to make my life easier. Rather than focusing on Seamus, though, I decided to think about the exploding accessory market for children. After all, it's already way far ahead of the handheld device accessory market. I suppose this can be attributed to the fact that children have been around for a few thousand years longer than BBs. Oh, and yes, we're sort of concerned about the children's well-being and safety and blah blah blah. Even so, with all of the silly accessories that have come along during the past 20 years of overactive, over-involved, and overspending parenting, there are still items that have been overlooked.

Parents of babies and toddlers are mostly craving some sort of containment device. Containment of the actual child unit, yes, but also of the free-flowing bodily fluids that accompany said child. Oh, and their stuff. They have lots and lots of stuff.

Some ideas:
* No piece of children's clothing should be unreversible.
* Kid's underpants should come with a removable lining—about 10 layers deep.
* Stores shouldn't sell mittens without strings to the parent of any child under the age of 12. If they all wore them, the geek factor would wear off and we could spend hours less at the

school lost and found, or the bargain bins at Walmart. Come to think of it, can we do the same for tiny hockey gloves?

• Glass partitions between rows in a van would be very helpful.

• As would blinders to prevent young riders from noticing the fast-food outlets we pass. These could also work to stop the viewing of portable DVD movies by motion-sickness-inclined children (and never mind the piece of chocolate Mom is silently chewing in the front row).

• Boots with combination locks.

• Snotproof sleeves.

• Marker-resistant leather couches.

• The agreement by all toy manufacturers to include extras of the little pieces of plastic they know we're going to break off while trying to transform that Transformer from an ice cream truck to the abominable snowman . . . the first time we do it.

Postscript

For non-users of either toddlers or BBSPs, it may seem like a natural to combine the two and have the BB *become* an accessory for a child. For example, you might be thinking you could allow the toddler to use the BB for a quick, distracting game of BrickBreaker. This is an amateur's mistake. Do not allow access! If your child loves the BB (or BrickBreaker, or both), you'll never get it back. If he hates it, he'll throw it on the ground and you won't want to be held responsible for your actions after that. This blog explores how BBSPs and children are alike . . . not how to bring the two of them together. Give your head a shake.

Tags: Unnatural combo. Containment.

May 15
Pay Attention, New or Recycled Modern Mummies!

Can't get my head out of the accessory thing, really.

The last two decades have produced the "wet wipe warmer" and the "enviro-bags" you *should* buy for your baby's used diapers. (For a complete list see my first book, *The Secret Life of Supermom*.) I have had fun buying, trying, and generally ridiculing most of these. There is one item, however, that I do not consider to be an accessory. It's a necessity. Oddly, I find that this parenting aid is being questioned in this new age of modern parenting. The bouncy chair? Nope. The swimming diaper? Guess again, but you're getting closer. It's the "real" diaper! There is a new league of parents who call themselves "diaper-free" (I believe the word "society" is attached to this moniker, but they already sound weird and cult-like and not very societal, if you ask me). So here it is: We're not talking about diaper-free once the child in question is three years old, as in my house and many others, but rather diaper-free *always*. From birth. No shit. Or, actually, the reverse.

Okay. Now that you've had a chance to really wrap your head around this, I'll continue. Apparently, the belief is that parents who are attuned to their babies' needs can intuitively tell when their darlings are going to have a #1 or #2. It's just a matter of looking for the right signals and then getting said baby on the toilet, potty, paper bag ... some waste receptacle ... in time for little Stinky to freely release their burden, without the constraints and tyranny of diapers. *Ha ha ha ha ha ha ha ha!*

Sorry. Seriously. With all four of my kids, it seemed to me that the babies surprised even themselves when they peed. How the hell was *I* supposed to know when they were going to do it? Let's take a closer look at this, folks. Aren't these diaper-free zealots advocating training the parent, not the child? And aren't we truly going through enough life changes just with having the baby in the first place? Have we not given 99.9% of our lives over to this magical creature, without being made to feel guilty about setting up a containment device for its waste? It already owns us. Handing over control of this particular baby-related activity seems absolutely ludicrous. The moment the child is born we hand over our souls, our hearts, and our minds. Do we really have to hand over the ability to more or less choose when we wipe up their feces? (Come on, except when it's your first-born, you know you can let any baby wallow in their deposits for as long as it takes to at least finish that important phone call or cup of coffee.)

Being a cynical sort of bitch, I'm naturally curious about the crossover appeal of the "diaperless infant" and the "family bed." Based on my vivid and visual imagination (meconium is just not going to come out of those Egyptian sheets), I would venture that maybe the appeal isn't too high, although there is a certain mindset that lends itself to either decision. You know, being diaper-less is really all about handing your life over. With the family bed in the mix you can throw your sex life in there, too. Yes, I was once childless too and I know you can have sex in places other than your bed. But parents, speak up, please: When was the last time you had unplanned sex on the kitchen table or the basement couch?

Tags: Losers. Wipers.

May 20
Mother's Day

With all these accessory thoughts crowding my head, I almost forgot to share my thoughts on Mother's Day. (I know, I know, you're *so* glad I remembered, right?!)

Most moms know (or at least figure out eventually) that Mother's Day is actually not about them, but about the kids. My Mother's Day went something like this: The kids made their lovely heartfelt handmade cards (I'm trying really hard not to notice that the picture they drew of me includes a blonde moustache and a massive ass) and then presented me with a teacher-written "Cuz I'm small" poem. They had tucked these treasures on a tray, burned some toast with Daddy's help, and slopped orange juice all the way up my newly carpeted stairs ("winter white"—what was I thinking?). They shook me awake (totally unnecessary as the youngest had already tripped on my discarded clothes and head butted me in the stomach), dumped the whole thing on my bed, and announced "Happy Mother's Day!" Which was quickly followed by, "Eat the toast eat the toast eat the toast" and "my present's the best right? Right? Right? He's hitting me! You're going to die you little booger!" . . . and then it really started to degenerate.

I love my kids. I love that they love Mother's Day. But they just don't get it sometimes. My perfect Mother's Day would involve me, my bed, maybe a coffee, and my beloved Seamus. Call me a mean old cynic if you want to, but isn't this day supposed to be all about us? Mostly, I want to forget, just for a few lovely hours, that I am defined as being a mother.

I've told my husband for years not to buy me anything for Mother's Day—from him, via the kids, or any combination thereof. I'm *not* his Mother, and I find it kind of creepy. I once had a male friend justify it by saying, "But she's the mother of my children." Oh, really. They're now divorced. I wonder if he still buys the present—she's still the mother of his children, after all.

Which leads me to consider why Seamus is a more welcome guest in my bedroom on Mother's Day morning than my other children:

• The aforementioned juice spilling and requisite burnt-toast eating is eliminated.

• It's quiet. It buzzes. I tap. It's quiet.

• It's not sticky. Usually.

• It provides me with adult conversation instead of forcing me to pull apart two warring preschoolers while sitting in a bed, trapped by a tippy, sloppy tray. "I love you both, goddammit. Now go and see your father!"

• It doesn't ask "Is Mother's Day over now?", "Why isn't there a BB day?", "Can you help Dad start the dishwasher?", and "What can we do while Dad is working on the computer"?

And most of all, there's no cleanup required—emotionally or physically.

Tags: Its. All. About. Me.

May 22
Fun and Upgrades

I've had my new toy—I mean, technological advancement—for five months now, and I'm happy to report that I've completely mastered its common, everyday uses (email, online shopping, BrickBreaker, et cetera). Now the fun can really begin! I can turn my attention to finding less obvious, but just as useful, applications. Allow me to provide some examples:

1. When planning on attending a wedding or Bar Mitzvah, pre-program the email addresses of the other attendees into a handy distribution list. Then, just when the ceremony is at a crucial stage, send an email to the gang to see whom you can "out" (i.e., who's looking at their Berry when they're not supposed to). Make sure the email reads something like "Shame on you." (In the body of the message that is; the subject should be something racy like "Me. You. My Tongue.")

2. Set your alarm to go off right in the middle of a meeting you know is going to bore you to tears. Others will think it's your phone ringing. This will allow you to mutter something along the lines of, "Sorry, sick kid" and dash out.

3. Send an email to your spouse at lunchtime. Since he never tires of telling you how he spends his lunch hours chained to his desk eating crappy mystery-meat sandwiches (and not lounging in chic downtown restaurants with skanky co-workers) he had better reply ASAP and there had better not be any spelling mistakes. Make sure the subject line reads, "Oh, poor

you" or, "Just wanted to brighten your day" to ensure the guilt quotient is turned up really high.

4.   Email someone else in the stands at your child's hockey game. If she answers, you have a new friend. If she ignores the vibration to watch her 6-year-old stumble down the ice, back away slowly.

5.   The next time you're out on a "Ladies Night" (which involves alcohol, of course), email your husbands with a naughty suggestion and see which hubby responds first. Loser has to buy the next round. Now try emailing each other's husbands (under your own name) with a slightly lewd suggestion and see which one comes back with the best response. Winner gets a bottle of wine. Loser has to book some therapy and get a lawyer on speed dial.

6.   Borrow someone's BBSP on the pretence of using their cellphone. Make up an excuse—like your kid has a fever of 101 and you have to call home to check in (such a caring and selfless Mom, seriously). Then email a booty call to people on the owner's address list. Even if you don't get to see the responses, the BB owner will. Fun and hilarity should ensue.

7.   Send a suggestive note to a man who has the same first name as your husband. Quickly follow it up with another note two minutes later that says "Oh, sorry, did you read that?" You'll accomplish two things: 1) a man you know (besides said husband) will think you're hot, and 2) you just might get an unexpected offer . . .

Yes, you too can have hours of fun (at the expense of others) with your BB. Clip this list and put it in your wallet as a reminder that others may also have read this blog. You don't want to fall for that tongue note, do you? Already did? Sorry, sweetie.

Tags: Fun. Fun. Fun. Sorry.

May 24
RIM People, Pay Attention

If I could convince the New Product people at RIM to devise upgrades for my BlackBerry smartphone, I wouldn't have to manufacture my own entertainment at the expense of others. Here's some free market insight and research for you, RIM folks: Berry-Head Moms need their very own upgrades. You see us in the mall, on the street, in playgrounds, coffee shops—anywhere a "stay-at-home-mom" is likely to be when she's not at home (which is almost always). Mostly, we're busy emailing friends, catching up on gossip, or booking the occasional bit of work. I was more than a little disappointed the other day when I read that RIM's latest BlackBerry smartphone upgrades would include an MP3 player, a camera, and other things I just didn't want or need. It got me thinking about the upgrades Moms could actually use. Music and photos have their place, but I'd really like to see the following improvements:

1. *Calorie counter:* Simply wave food in front of the BB to activate an automatic calorie calculation and running tally. When the pre-programmed daily total is reached, the unit will shock its owner repeatedly until the food item is put down. I need this kind of motivation (don't judge me!). I'm already using Seamus as a sort of "fat judge"—I take note of the amount of pain I'm in when I bend over and the holster clip digs into my muffin-top fat (perched on top of my inappropriately low-slung jeans)—so this calorie-counter idea is a natural progression, right?

2. *Electronic remote:* Use this to turn on the oven, dishwasher, roving vacuum cleaner—any number of household appliances that might need to be turned on, or off, while I'm enjoying that last coffee at Starbucks, or that first glass of wine at Cathy's down the street.

3. *Pager:* A gimme. How many of us have dropped our BBs while bending over to tie up little shoes, pick up squealing brats, or tidy up assorted dirty clothes? Reaching for your little friend and finding the holster empty is almost as worrying as reaching for a little hand that suddenly isn't there.

4. *Breathalyzer:* Yes, for those aforementioned little glasses of char at Cathy's. While she's just a quick walk down the street, chances are you're not going straight home after you've unloaded a week's worth of gossip. No, you're probably hopping into your minivan to pick up some kid from some lesson someplace. Wouldn't it be good to know where you stand?

5. *Personalized tones/vibrations:* I need to know when Kerry down the street has put on 10 pounds but is still stuffing herself into her "skinny jeans." I need to know this right away. I don't need to know that the school is holding yet another fundraiser and I've been nominated to find silent auction items—again.

6. *Homing signal from husband's BBSP:* Notification that hubby is five minutes away from home would give us, ummm, multi-tasking Moms time to fire up the vacuum, make those lines in the carpet, stow the wine glasses, pitch the trashy magazines, and make like we're folding laundry. A bit of a twist on the "boss plus five" rule.

7. *Listening/recording device:* This would come in handy when the gossip is just too good and too unbelievable. Often I am too distracted by bleeding children or speeding cars to take in every word of the daily news dispersed during the early-

morning bus stop confab. Having a microphone to pick up every intonation and damning word would be of assistance when trying to responsibly pass along these little nuggets.

8. *Adjustable vibration intensity:* Turn up the vibration intensity and you've got yourself a handy little personal massager. Place it on the belt by your lower back and you may never want to get off that park bench again.

Pay attention, progressive technology engineers. Wait. Did I just use the phrase "progressive technology engineers?" Ah, what the hell, this is all fantasy anyway. You mythical creatures need to know the modern-mom user is a growing market segment. You want to make sure we're happy. Have you seen what a bunch of *unhappy* moms look like? Have you heard them? There's no volume control. Just hang around any indoor playground or park in the early afternoon (otherwise known as "pre-meltdown" time) and you'll see what I mean. We'll be the ones flapping our gums or tapping away on our BBs—sometimes at the same time.

Tags: Patent pending. Again.

May 25
Speaking of Areas for Improvement

I've already mused about the potential for BBSP upgrades. Now, after spending an endless P.D. day with my four children, it occurs to me what a great thing it would be if children could also be upgraded. Not that the little angels aren't near enough perfection (like when they're sleeping, or in retrospect), but can't all of us use a little self-improvement? A volume control, a "mute" button, hell, even an "on/off" switch would be welcome in most households, with kids of any age. For teenagers, the addition of a circuit that could "power off" rolling eyes, sneers, scoffs, and general physical admonitions toward parents would be particularly helpful in maintaining family peace and serenity. Unfortunately, without contravening pesky little things like ethics, child development, and oh . . . I don't know . . . the law, this won't be possible in our lifetime. The best we can do is repeat the veteran parent's mantra: "It's just a phase. It's just a phase." And invest in a good pair of earplugs.

Tags: Teenagers. Lovely.

May 26
Nirvana? Not So Fast.

Back to those moms tapping away in the playground. Listen up again, RIM. What if there were some way to combine reading and the wonder of the BlackBerry smartphone into a trashy e-novel you could read in instalments? Am I the only one who just got goosebumps? (I have to admit to visions of the *Seinfeld* episode where George tries unsuccessfully to combine sex, eating, and sports—the ultimate male triumvirate.)

I know that the e-book concept has been around for some years now, with tech companies promoting the possibility of carrying as many as 80 books on your handheld. For fairly obvious reasons (tiny print, battery sucking, scorched eyeballs) this development has never really taken off. Improvements in font size, brightness, and battery consumption/capability were supposed to have corrected this apparent oversight in the readers' market. They haven't. Could it be that perhaps only "important" works of fiction or non-fiction were being developed as possible "content" for handheld devices? It has been my experience that BB users have notoriously short attention spans—hello, they can't even finish a face-to-face conversation without looking at their BBs. The interruptions one would face while trying to get through even a page (let alone a chapter) of something that has to hang together with some cohesion, like, say, a novel, might be insurmountable. I therefore beg these e-book providers to hook up with RIM and consider the following shorter titles, and to send them to us in bite-sized emails:

- *Tips for Healthy Living in the Limelight*, by Amy Winehouse, Lindsay Lohan, and Pete Doherty. Intro by Britney Spears.
- *Sure-fire Methods to Stop Your Children from Swearing in Front of Condescending Relatives and Neighbours.*
- *How to Make Thong Underwear Comfortable.*
- *Reasons Men Are Hot When They Watch Sports All Weekend.*
- *Thinking of Having a Seventh Child? Some Benefits.*

The BB-toting modern mom may not be ready for *War and Peace* yet, but she just might be ready for a few minutes of peace and quiet to enjoy some light reading while tuning out the warring children in front of her.

Tags: Thongs. Hot. Swearing.

June 3
Efficiency Is Key

It's true that while the thrill of the buzzing BB can't be topped by, well, *anything* (except sex in the first few weeks of a relationship—and even then you might sneak a look), the kind folk at RIM are busy developing new and useful ways for us to receive information.

The ability to surf the Net (www.perezhilton.com is especially entertaining during school concerts), review documents, look at PDFs, send directory information back and forth—all of these are wonderful. And now comes the news that an airline has just introduced advanced flight check-in via your handheld device! No more lining up at the electronic kiosk just to join another line to drop bags. This is progress? We can now check in *while* we're in line. As usual, this tidbit of news got me thinking about how the BBSP might allow us to bypass other machines that cause us frustration in our daily lives. ATMs, driver's license kiosks, and any sort of government-installed machine spring immediately to mind.

To take this one step further, I think it would be great to bypass *any* lineup simply because I'm holding onto Seamus. For instance, registering for children's sports lessons and camps. Is there really a more annoying lineup than this? Before you answer, consider the company you keep in these situations. There's, "Well, little Johnny was A-level last year so I'm sure they'll be begging to have him back," and "I need to speak with the counsellor to make sure they understand the intricacies involved with supervising a sensitive and special child like my Willow." If we all used our BBs to enter our main personality characteristic (come on, admit to "overbearing," you hockey mom!) along with a description of our kid (the words "perfect" and "gifted" would not be allowed), we could make this whole process faster by splitting into shorter lines and finding our own kind.

Think about it. Any place in which you require information immediately—how long the wait in the doctor's office is going to be, whether the new gynecologist is cute, or even a lie detector (for children, insincere friends, and vacant husbands)—would be good. Note of caution: The lie-detector feature would have to come with a warning about not asking the universally badly answered questions of "Do I look fat in this?" "Do you think Jim's new wife is really all that cute?" or "Do you really like sports better than you like me?"

Tags: Men. Lies. Lines.

June 7
Hide Away, My Good Man

Okay, it's been about four weeks since the sheets on my bed were changed. Why do I own this chore? I'd pass it off to my husband if only I could find the bugger. What is he hiding from, the washing machine? From the chore itself? From me? Seems it might be possible, given what I read in the newspaper a month ago as I was searching for Mr. Sneaky. The headline screamed: "Male need to hide from women only natural." Really! Well, guess what? Sometimes they want to hide, and sometimes we just want them to go away. But *not* when the dishwasher needs emptying, the laundry has been sitting in the dryer for a week, and the kids are screaming for dinner.

There have been many theories as to why men disappear— heading off to look for quiet bonding places either alone or with their male compatriots. My husband attended an all-boy's camp for a month each summer, a tradition we have passed on to our own 13-year-old son. And the best part, according to him? "No girls." Probably in his case he means "No sisters and moms."

Anthropologists might suggest this desire to retreat and re-group, away from women, is a hold over from the days when men felt a need to bond before entering a fight. This modern-day observer suggests that it is a reconditioned response to a world in which men are actually expected to participate in child rearing and domestic duties (like changing the frigging sheets! Okay, I know I need to let that go). Consider also:

"Mom, can you help me put together this Lego castle?"
"Go and ask your Dad."
"But he just went into the bathroom . . . I can't wait that long!"

Or

"Mom, can you take me and my friends to the mall?"
"Go and ask your Dad."
"But he went to Home Depot and you know he'll be there all morning."

Or even:

"Mom, wipe my bum!"
"Where is your Dad?"
"Mom, wipe my bum!!"
"Where is your Dad?"
"Mom, the floor needs wiping too!"*

* Dad is later observed crouching in front of his favourite bush in the backyard, rubbing soil between his fingers. He does this for 27 minutes.

So what's going on here? It's not as though the men have never pulled some of their own domestic weight, it's just that in the past, this has been a reactive/defensive measure against their wives' nagging, threats, and holdouts. (Is there anything more annoying than a man standing in front of you on a Saturday morning asking, "So, what can I help you with?") These days, however, they are expected to not only shoulder the chores, but also own a few. For some of these Neanderthals, it's simply too much, as my crunchy pillowcases will attest. Let me explain.

After reading that article back in early May, I decided to confront my own hide-away male. I spoke calmly and rationally about the challenges of trying to keep a house clean with four children while he indulged his workaholic habit. He graciously agreed to take on the one task for which my level of disdain was matched only by its necessity: The aforementioned changing of the sheets. For five beds. Naturally, at the time of this discussion, the chore in question needed doing, hence the top-of-mindness it had for me at that moment. Men may be surprised to discover that women do not harbour glamorous thoughts of cleaning and tidying at all times.

Cue the tiptoe music and the shadow of a sneaky male. That was four weeks ago. Yep. Four entire weeks have passed since he agreed to "handle it." Yesterday morning, I finally snapped. I couldn't take it anymore (and frankly, the hard pillowcases were a bit of a turnoff). I washed the damn sheets. When he came home and discovered that I had done so, his reaction was, "Oh, I was going to do that." Uh huh. And tonight, he brought home flowers. Score! While I haven't actually managed to release this chore with any great success, I still succeeded. The flowers tell me that I've gotten him to take on the *guilt* of the chore, which is just as much "work" as the chore itself. He *owns* that frigging sheet-laundering process now.

Now, if only I could *find* him, I'd get him to start scheduling the children's summer camp programs. As if.

Tags: Can run. Can never hide.

June 12
Helloooo? Is Anybody Out There?

Why doesn't she answer my email? Did I piss her off? Was it my tone? Was there a tone? I ask myself this question about a million times a week now that I live in the wonderful world of instantaneous communication. I now have the ability to send and receive emails that are read and responded to immediately. *Most of the time.* The most frustrating thing an avid BBSP user like myself can face is dealing with unacknowledged email. If you send an email, and no one reads it, does it really exist? Is there such a thing as a truly deleted email? We've all read stories about letters that went missing during the war, only to be discovered stuffed behind an old mail desk that hadn't been cleaned in more than 80 years. (If only the letter had been delivered, the correspondents would have a) gotten married, b) broken up, c) had that baby after all, or d) stayed in Europe and tried the bratwurst.) But what about lost emails, or emails never read by the intended recipient? As frightening as it can be to hit "send" and realize I've entered the wrong email address (automatic addressing can be a scary thing), I usually discover what I've done. The unlucky recipient is often kind enough to send it back to me with some snarky note: "Thanks for calling me your love muffin, but I think you meant another Dave. I am, however, available at 3:00."

Unlike these potentially awkward situations, not knowing if someone has read my email and is deliberately not responding can be as angst inspiring as waiting for that Grade 8 boy to call me back after I left him a message about my upcoming party.

For the recipient, the unread email is a thing of beauty. You have all the power. Someone has reached out to you, and you get to decide whether to read it, respond, or pretend it went into the ether (particularly recommended if that guy you dated in Grade 8 has tracked you down—from prison). On the other hand, you don't want to attach a "receipt requested" tag to every email you send—in fact, you don't want to attach a "receipt requested" tag to *any* email you send. This is the act of the truly pathetic. One option might be to ignore emails from the same recipient once she does deign to answer, just to show her what it's like, but first you need to know her ERT (Estimated Response Time). Here's how it works: If a recipient's ERT is anything like mine (under 1.2 seconds), and I don't get an immediate response, I assume that she is either driving, in the middle of an invasive medical procedure, or dead. (Honestly, she's probably not driving . . . at least not on a road where there are red lights, at any rate.) If her ERT is more like minutes (what is she doing that is so important?) I give her up to half a day before I really start to feel insecure and unloved, or guilty about having offended her with my unintended "tone."

I simply do not understand people who can take up to a week (a week, I know, seriously!) to respond to any sort of email. Even if it's an invite to a Tupperware party, I answer right away (the answer is easy, though, I'll admit). No, I'm not a trader on Wall Street or Bay Street, and I'm not closing that super-big deal, but the current North American lifestyle is based on immediate gratification, which is why the BBSP is perfect! Add in the fact that I *hate* to walk anywhere and mistakenly burn calories, and the ability to send a message to the guy sitting in the next cubicle, down the road, or even in the next room (come on, it's a long walk to my family room from here) becomes even more attractive.

Tags: ERT. Hey, you!

June 15
Protect Yourself from the Overprotective

It's the early part of the new millennium, and the Overprotective Parent is enjoying the benefits of a litigious, blame-throwing, finger-pointing, and study-intensive society. Want to go tobogganing down that neighbourhood hill? Take your helmet. How about skating on the pond? A helmet. Skateboarding? Helmet. Scooter? Helmet. Walking across the plush carpeting in your four-bedroom suburban home? Helmet—after all, that side table has some nasty-looking edges. But protectiveness over physical activity is just the tip of the overprotective iceberg. The words "shut up" and "stupid" are apparently now "swear words." I don't know where the Society for the Determination of Obscenities meets, but you can bet your peanut-free ass that it's run by an OP (Overprotective Parent. Come on, people, get with the program.). In the world of the OP, seemingly innocuous things, events, situations, and yes, even words, can take on a health-hazarding or potentially ego-diminishing power. Here are a few scenarios to help you decide whether you are an OP, or if you have a firm grip on reality. If more than two of these situations sound familiar, you might want to consider counselling.

• You put your 5-year-old in a stroller to take her for the five-minute walk to kindergarten. She might wear out her legs on the way there. Never mind the 3.2 kilometre circuit she just ran from the kitchen, through the living room, into the front hall, and back again. She needs to save her strength for carpet time.

- You put sunscreen on your child when he's going on an all-day field trip to an indoor museum.
- You make your child wear a sweater when *you're* cold.
- You won't sign your son up for Cub Scouts because there is "something wrong with the men who want to be involved with young boys."
- Your child is 17 and you're still worried about trying her with peanut butter. (She's already gotten stoned, trust me. The peanut butter will not be a biggie.)
- You ask 12 other parents about the suitability of the JK teacher, just in case junior gets off on the wrong foot (like, maybe he'll glue something on wrong?).
- You follow your 14-year-old daughter into public restrooms to make sure the stall is clean first.
- You pack a snack for a 15-minute park visit. Something healthy, of course.
- You cut the chicken off the chicken wing bone so that Junior won't choke. He's 9.
- You won't let any of your children go on a field trip unless you are chaperoning. None of them is under the age of 10.

The OP is a fact of life in today's world. The key to overcoming this plague is to search out a notable OP, follow her for a week, and then make sure that you do not repeat any of her behaviours. If you *ever* find yourself starting a sentence with, "Well, that might work for other kids, but I find my child is oversensitive . . . ," it's kinda over for you. An alternative strategy might be to align yourself with an OP, display some horrendous parenting behaviour (e.g., letting your child walk 100 feet ahead of you on the sidewalk, or packing her a pre-made "Lunch Mate" without adding fresh fruit) and hope that she is conscious-bound to take over responsibility for the well-being of your child. Not as far-fetched as you think. The truly OPs love to share their parenting strategies with other parents, particularly OPs in training, so demonstrating the "bad example" in person simply lends credence to the fact that they are absolutely justified in their own over-the-top behaviour. It also explains why she had to quit her full-time job. And it fully supports her "Thank god I'm at home with the children or I don't know how we'd manage" argument. You get some free babysitting, your child comes to see you as actually being "normal" (as if you care), and if something goes terribly, terribly wrong while your child is in her care (like they find an axe in the basement and start swinging it), you can feed off that faux pas for months. It's all good. Keep your friends close; keep the OP even closer. That is, in fact, if you can get them to look up from the treasure that is their child and actually pay attention to what you're saying.

As a seasoned veteran of the playground wars, I'd like to share some of my own survival tips. Because I'm mean, all involve toying with Ms. Helicopter (think hovering) for my own amusement. Enjoy!

- "Did you hear about Janie's little girl? She's only 2 and she could run rings around that little kid over there. Oh, that's yours? Bless her."
- "There's a new study out that links time spent away from parents with increased independence and risk taking. It's fascinating how your son can hold on to your leg, suck his thumb, and hold his blanket all at the same time. I didn't know 10-year-olds were so dextrous!"
- "I heard that our kids' new teacher was let go from her last school for not enforcing carpet time. Honestly."

- "Did you hear about Room 604's disastrous Cupcake Day? They'll never live it down. No icing *or* sprinkles. Seriously."
- "I've heard that when the school bus drops the kids off, there is no official supervision from the bus to the front door, which is a good six feet away. I'm starting a petition to have the principal personally escort them. Wanna sign it? If this isn't already in her job description, it should be."

Trying to have a conversation with an OP is like to trying to stand between a man and the Home Depot flyer. You just won't register, and in the end, it just doesn't matter. You didn't actually want to be friends, did you? Did you?

Tags: Get a life.

June 17
Father's Day

I joked on Mother's Day that Seamus (unlike kids) doesn't ask, "Why isn't there a BB Day?" Well, today I'm thinking maybe we could just rename Father's Day "BB Day" and we wouldn't have to deal with organizing a whole new holiday.

Don't get me wrong. I love men. Generally speaking, and in theory. But specifically . . . well, just like with anything you get too close to, the warts start to show.

Ask a man what he's thinking about—go ahead, I dare ya. I already know he'll respond with one of two possible answers.

1. "Nuthin."
2. "If I wanted you to know, I'd be talking."

The great thing about a BB is, they don't think. They reflect back everything you want to know—via the Internet, the gossipy emails from your girlfriends, or the reminder note that you have a pedicure scheduled for right now.

After the first flush of romance, men forget. They forget your birthday, your anniversary, the perfume you wear (do you wear perfume?), whether your ears are pierced, that special place you had lunch, "your" song, hell, even your first name when they're being flirted with by a tip-hungry waitress.

A BB never forgets (unless you dunk the whole thing in a glass of wine); one of its main attributes is that it serves as a reminding device. Appointments buzz you, friends beep you, calls come in . . . it's all good.

A BB doesn't put on weight or stick his hands down his keyboard while watching TV. Beeps, vibrations, and ring tones are the only bodily functioning sounds it emits. It doesn't "turn off" in the middle of a conversation, and it never tells you you're too old to wear that.

Granted, the "shoulders" on Seamus aren't quite man-sized enough for me, but I'm waiting for that accessory add-on as well.

Tags: Men. BBs. No contest.

June 20
It's a Time/Distance/Speed Thing

Six months in with Seamus and here's what I've learned: lazy, fat, "do it now," immediate-gratification-addicted North Americans are the perfect target market for this little piece of technological heaven. I was surprised to read today, however, that RIM is looking at Africa as the next big growth area. Don't get me wrong, I think BB world domination is a fabulous idea—I just have the impression that things move at a, well, more leisurely pace in Africa.

Of course, this got me thinking. North Americans are often accused of living in a 24/7 society, with Sunday store openings, all-night bars, overscheduled children, and overworked parents. The BlackBerry smartphone is the perfect tool for this lifestyle. There may, however, be entire segments of this society—or entire professions, more to the point—for which the BBSP is not well suited. I'm thinking, for example, of any professions that does not require speed and time-effectiveness as part of its mandate (unlike the hockey mom, who is simultaneously trying to get through rush-hour traffic, encourage her kids to stuff down their dinner prior to arriving at the arena, and remind them to try to wash their hair in the shower as she can't remember the last time that mop saw moisture that wasn't generated from the body under it). Occupations that seem not to operate on speed or efficiency might include:

- The doctors at any shopping-mall medical centres. First,

the wait ("Oh, nurse? Mark my age up by a year on that form, would you? I entered it when I first got here") and then the, "Well, I'm pretty sure this is poison ivy but I'm just going to consult a book—I'll be right back." (Here's a hint doc: Don't tell me you're going to look it up. I already suspect you graduated in the bottom half of your class. You work *here*, instead of at a real practice, for a start, and you're in your 50s.)

• Teachers and certain parents engaged in the "15-minute" parent/teacher conference. The teacher needs to ensure that the parents totally understand how he has the hardest job in the world under the worst possible circumstances. One parent can't wait to get out of this boring meeting and answer the emails that have been buzzing in for the last 15 minutes. Unfortunately, he/she is sitting next to a spouse who wants to talk about ways to improve Janie's self-esteem, social confidence, and studying habits, and how the curriculum needs to be improved. What can we do to work together? Give me strength.

• The bartender at a theatre. You only have 20 minutes to throw back a large glass of wine before sitting through another excruciating 2 1/2 hours of the unedited version of Mozart's *Magic Flute* done by a second-rate opera company in which the women aren't even fat. And you need to pee. And you're sitting next to an asshole.

• Any government official in any official capacity where they can make you sweat and confess just by waiting. Passport control, customs, driver's license clerks, airport security (yes, please keep my poor Seamus inside that X-ray machine just another 10 minutes or so to really get me worried and forget about the illegal nail scissors I have in my carry-on bag), embassies, even the postal carrier who's waiting for you to sign for a completely unexpected and mysterious registered letter.

- The clerk at the gas station who can't quite seem to get the Visa terminal to work correctly and who insists on signing up every customer for a valuable points program through a convenient 27-question form. Meanwhile, you're cursing yourself for making this the first time you've ever left your sleeping baby alone in the unguarded minivan. He's sure to be stolen at any second.

- The flipping cable guy, appliance repair and delivery people, telephone installer and any other service personnel who cannot commit to being at your house in anything smaller than an eight-hour window. No, please, take your time with that smoke outside my house; I'm sure there are far more important things on your list.

Modern Moms know that time and speed are crucial requirements for getting anything done with children; if you slow down or falter for even a nanosecond, they will be all over you like dads on a swimsuit edition.

Getting them dressed (hurry!), out the door (come on!), into the van (chop, chop!) is essential for keeping Mom's sanity as she realizes every moment spent with them is a moment less lingering over a latte at Starbucks. Ah wait, there's that thrilling buzz beneath her Lululemon yoga pants. At her waistband. *From the BB.* (This is a PG book, people!) While some of us have a somewhat sexual attachment to our BlackBerrys, as far as I know, there haven't yet been any sexual attachments made *for* a BB. Not that I've been researching that or anything.

Tags: Speed. Cable guy. Hahahahahaha.

June 21
"Vacation" Time

Only a week until school ends, and then the vacation begins. Wait, I think I actually have that backward.

Unfortunately, one thing that never really goes out of style (or becomes any more pleasant) is the family vacation. Once the summer "break" rolls around, many of us parents will find ourselves strapping in for the wildest ride of our lives. And it's not the upside-down roller coaster at the nearby amusement park. It's a six-to-ten hour drive in the family van, where no one is safe, and everyone is under attack—both verbally and physically (in a bodily fluid sort of way). Last year, I thought I had discovered the ultimate in distraction technology (no, it wasn't a BBSP for kids). I should have known it would prove to be too good to be true. But I'm getting ahead of myself. Let's start at the beginning.

So you've finalized the spreadsheet—detailing which child can sit in which seat, with which seat partner—that will take you down the driveway without a fight . . . maybe. I recently heard of a study that said that the average family can drive for only 12 minutes without an argument breaking out. Me? I'm thrilled to hit 12 *seconds*, which will take me to the end of the cul de sac.

The real boredom sets in at the predetermined 13-second mark. Now, in the past, I have prepared "treat bags," brought juice boxes, favourite toys, et cetera, but none of these seemed to hold any long-term appeal. So, you might understand why

I was positively giddy when we purchased a minivan that came with built-in DVD player, complete with headphones! With children ranging in age from 4 to 15, I was dreaming about the insightful and adult conversations my husband and I would have in the front row while the children sat zombie-like in the back, engrossed in the latest family comedy. Our contented murmurings, I imagined, would be interrupted only by the cheerful giggles of an appreciative and content audience. You know what? No.

Here are the lessons I've learned about the joys of having a DVD in your car or van. I happily share them with you, and with any car manufacturer executives who might happen to be reading.

1.   The headphones are expensive and usually don't work properly. Don't let the expensive price tag fool you into thinking you're getting a quality piece of electronic equipment. After approximately 10 minutes during which the headphones did provide sound (as we drove out of the dealership parking lot), they were otherwise employed as projectile ammunition in the war zone that is the back row. And they gobble up expensive little batteries that gleefully run out overnight. I believe the manufacturers installed an "on" button that is self-regulating. And possessed.

2.   The movie choice itself is problematic. Give me one movie that kids aged 4, 8, 13, and 15 can all agree on that doesn't result in the preschoolers learning useful expressions like "booty-licious" or "yo Mamma," or force teenagers to sing songs like "Death to Barney."

3.   There are side effects. Apparently, hurtling down a highway at 120 km an hour while watching a stationary screen can

make one nauseous. Witnessing a seat partner being nauseous can make others feel the same way. Go figure.

4. It can be hard on adults. Musical movies, such as the ubiquitous and cloying *High School Musical* are their own unique type of torture when listened for the 14th time from the front seat. It's not great on the first pass, folks. Can't wait until they pop in the Hannah Montana/Miley Cyrus World Tour! What's more, my personal tolerance level for body part and washroom humour turns out to be quite low. This eliminates any Adam Sandler, Will Ferrell, Martin Lawrence, Eddie Murphy, or Pixar movie. My husband's tolerance, on the other hand, remains remarkably high.

5. It can change your perspective. After listening to hours of *The Wiggles, Family Guy*, and *The Simpsons*, one can come to appreciate the droll wit and homoerotic relationship of SpongeBob and Squidward.

So, I've given up on the utopia of the perfect van ride and now spend my hours in the passenger seat composing letters to the three major car companies, asking them to install the ultimate in pimping out a kid-friendly ride: the middle-row glass partition. And head phones that just block *out* the noise. That don't need batteries.

As Jerry Seinfeld once stated, "There is no such things as Fun for the Whole Family." Deal with it.

Tags: Family fun. Yep.

June 23
The BlackBerry Smartphone, on "Vacation"

Planning a vacation? From what? The kids? Good luck—they'll probably want to tag along with you; likewise that pesky husband. And that BBSP will just keep on buzzing (god willing), no matter what you're doing. And yes, before you start sending comments by the thousands, I am aware of how truly pathetic it is to take Seamus to the beach, on a ski lift, up the side of a mountain, on a picnic, or even by the pool. Besides, none of these locations provides easy-to-access places for the BB to live. A bikini? Not unless the waistband is industrial strength (note to self: add idea to ongoing "accessories" list). So yes, taking your BB on vacation is pathetic. It's also necessary.

But you will need some preparation. Let's begin. You will be mocked. By friends, strangers, and relatives—those same kind people who mock you for giving your 2-year-old a bottle, for not breaking your 7-year-old's thumb-sucking habit and for allowing your 4-year-old to wear a diaper to bed at night. You know the correct retort: It starts with the word "Go" and ends with the word "yourself." Easy. But with BB mockers, you might need to get a little more creative. You need to have some standard explanations at the ready if you undertake the challenge of carrying your BB with you on vacation. Enter these into the "notepad" section of said device for easy reference.

• "My great-aunt Amelia is on death's doorstep and the doctor said he would email me if a life-support decision had to be made."

- "This? Oh, it's just for my kids. They can call me from the hotel room, the lobby, or the mall. You know teenagers; they really want us to know what they're up to all the time."
- "Oh, it's not work! No, no, no, no, no! That would be pathetic! No, this is simply to make sure I get to that macramé class on the beach on time. I love the alarm system. No, I haven't checked my emails at all! What kind of a loser do you think I am?"
- "I'm waiting for an important shipment from Paraguay. No, I can't tell you what it is."
- "My children's school is having a fundraiser the day after we get home and I want to make sure they receive all 27 of my handmade pencil cases. They're such a hit and I'd hate to disappoint the children."
- "This? Oh, it *looks* like a BlackBerry smartphone, but it's really a heart monitor. Don't tell my husband, I wouldn't want to upset him. The hospital custom-made it for me."
- "I'm tracking my calories on it. Cheesecake, anyone?"
- "I'm just using it to collect email addresses from all the fun people we've met on the cruise. Did I see you at the hairy chest contest? Did you win? It's Candace, right?"

If none of these retorts work, you can do what I keep threatening to do, and tuck your BB into a small fanny pack. This works for a number of reasons, the least of which is that no one will talk to the crazy person actually wearing a fanny pack. You can whip your BB out in elevators, in the washroom stall, behind the tiki tiki bar, and as soon as someone starts to approach, pop it back into the fanny pack and watch them retreat. Works like a charm. Bon voyage!

Tags: Fanny pack. Ewwww.

June 24
Countdown to Vacation Hell Continues

Yesterday I explored the challenges inherent in trying to smuggle a BBSP on vacation. Today, the topic is children. If you're taking a "family" vacation, the implication is that the "family" will actually be present—though I'm not sure from what, precisely, the average child needs a vacation. They're not escaping the laundry, the cooking, the deadly commute, or the backstabbing neighbours and colleagues. In fact, they're throwing themselves into the line of fire in that they'll be spending 24 hours a day for a number of days in a row with *their parents*, who already lose patience when forced to spend more than 10 minutes in the child's company (or is that just me?). What's going on here? What are they so happy about? Or is this the same type of self-delusion that parents succumb to when they think their family holiday will be idyllic, even though for the past seven months they've been threatening to send all of their holiday companions (including their spouse) away to military camp?

The sometimes great/sometimes horrifying thing about both children and BBs is that they remain pretty static, no matter the situation. If they (the children) have tantrums at home, they'll have them in Holland. If they don't like "foreign food" (which for some children is a taco) at home, they're certainly not going to like it in Mexico.

So what do you do if you are "caught" bringing small children on a holiday meant only for adults? As with the BBSP, you may want to consider the following plausible explanations for doing so (rather than sharing the fact that Jimmy Junior effectively eliminates the "holiday sex" which *some* women may be trying to avoid). Do yourself a favour and have the following arguments at the ready.

- "I read a study that indicated exposing a 2-year-old to high altitudes can eliminate all allergies for their whole life. Stowe, here we are! And the daycare is so reasonably priced! Hey, did you know I can get reception on my BB on this chairlift?"
- "Exposing my baby to fat hairy men in Speedos will burn the image into his brains (if not totally scarring his retinas) to the point where he will be unable to bring himself to perpetuate such a horror on any North American public beach in the future. Oooh, one in socks and sandals too! Bonus!"
- "Forcing my four children, aged 16 and under, to sit in a formal dining room three times a day will help them to develop a sophisticated palate . . . or at least to learn to play selections from Beethoven on varyingly filled water glasses."
- "The tour of the cognac factory is a terrific opportunity for the children to develop an appreciation of why it's a bad idea to start drinking before you're old enough to have permanently damaged your taste buds through smoking, hot chili pepper competitions, and that pickled-egg-eating contest at university."
- "I believe that museums should be living, breathing things, not stuffy monuments to days past (ack—stop trying grab the armless guy's penis, kids!). Children should be allowed to express their true response to art masterpieces, which may expose ancient scholars and jaded observers to a new light on old thinking (um, yes, that is a bunch of naked ladies showing off their bum-bums. Stop touching.)."

As mortifying as it is to have your children complain loudly about how boring the Louvre is, and how bad the food is at a European four-star, or laugh uproariously at the traditions and customs of a foreign land, you can save yourself some grief in these moments. If you're tapping away on Mr. BB, silently sharing your pain with your girlfriend back in Winnipeg, you may not hear all the whining. But be warned: If your child is attempting to share his own charming observation of the world while you are engaged, he will quickly lose any instilled sense of decorum and respect and raise his voice in a tone of righteous indignation. He may even shriek, "Mom! You brought Seamus to see the Mona Lisa?" Um, yep, I did. And I don't even have the excuse of having a built-in camera. But no one needs to know that.

So by all means venture forth on that holiday. Just remember that both the BB and the children will need periods of rest and recharging. Take my advice and make sure these activities don't happen at the same time. Don't worry: The quiet tap-tap-tapping on that tiny keyboard will never wake them up.

Tags: Vacation. Hell. Redundant.

July 15
Ascent into Hell (a.k.a. Being "Out of Range")

I've just spent three weeks travelling in France—with my four children. Lots to catch up on (i.e., complain about). It isn't bad enough that my children behave exactly the same way abroad as they do at home (and no, it's not exemplary behaviour, thanks for asking). While away—and therefore "out in public"—I have to pretend to discipline them in a kind and constructive sort of way, versus the screaming, humiliation, and threats I normally employ. In trying times at home I always have my BB to turn to. I can take a breath mid-screech, grope for the BB, and read a note that is either interesting (work related), inspiring (platitudes about work), or intriguing (gossip from the gals). Instantly, I am transported to a world where 4-year-olds at the grocery store knocking over trays of cream puffs with their big heads just don't exist—and, more importantly, don't matter. Not so while "out of range."

Being "out of range" is as frightening as starting your period in the middle of a summer patio party in your white sundress. You are totally without a net. And, to recap, no, I'm not a brain surgeon or a world leader, and countries and people would not be at fatal risk if I was out of contact with my "peeps." Still, I like to know that the people who want to stay in touch with me, can. As a self-employed writer, I'm only as relevant as the last piece I turned in. I just know that the minute my back (or "black") is turned, the much-sought-after-article for *Vogue* or *Time* will be requested. Or that guest appearance on *Oprah* or *The View*. Or, more likely, a request to speak at a staff meeting where my compensation is likely to be a Timbit.

But you get my point. Out of range sucks. Even in France.

Tags: Out of range. Arrrgh.

July 20
Vacations: The Perfect BlackBerry
Smartphone Opportunity . . . *Denied*!

Had to stop mid-rant the other day because of circumstances beyond my control. Let's just say it involved an unfortunate decision regarding allowing children to self-monitor their consumption of caffeinated pop and a permanently terrorized neighbourhood puppy. But never mind that, back to the whole vacation thing.

Please note that travel plans should never, ever be finalized until you have secured confirmation from your telecom provider that your BBSP will indeed work wherever you are going. Also, remember to pack a battery charger (there's nothing more irritating than a signal, but no strength) or a backup battery and the phone number for service, should you need it. I did none of these things, and found myself Berry-less for the duration. It was hell, and it robbed me of some fairly significant BB moments. For instance, I was unable to:

• Respond to editors and friends, "Sorry, can't access that file right now as I'm standing in the Louvre," or "Just testing to see if the signal works from the elevator in the Eiffel Tower," or even "Can anyone send me the French translation for 'Another cognac and order of truffles, please?'"
• Catch up on emails while stuck in hour-long lineups, on rainy boat cruises, or during lost hours by the hotel pool ("You kids can swim anywhere! We're in freaking Paris!").

- Tell my husband he has to take the toilet-paper-usage-challenged 4-year-old to the bathroom because I *must* get an email to this editor *right now* or I will lose a *huge* contract.
- Complain to my friends at home about my family and their annoying habits. What is it with my Mom having to read every frigging road sign out loud?
- Send annoying bragging emails such as "Do you think 40 Euros is a good price on an original French design?" or "What size are you again? There's a skirt here that's just faboo . . . if you respond in less than 10 minutes it's yours!" or "Sorry for not emailing sooner—you know what a constant diet of champagne does to me!"
- Play BrickBreaker during long plane rides, in airport lounges, or even on a cruise down the Seine in the rain. We all have our own ways to holiday.
- Stay in the loop with good neighbourhood gossip about the latest petitions started by the cow down the street. What if it's about me?

Faced with the lack of my handy BB as a method of distraction and entertainment, I was forced to rely on my children. It came as a pleasant surprise to discover a number of places where it was quite convenient (and entertaining) to have my children with me instead of safely stashed away at school or the babysitters.

Children have a delightful way of lowering the tone of any stuffy and pretentious outing. There's a certain pleasure that comes from thinking about abstractionist paintings—and the interpretations of life, death, struggle, mystery—while your 4-year-old loudly opines, "Look, Mom, I think someone threw a bucket of poo on that piece of white paper." I miss my children in situations where I'm forced to nod, smile politely, and not say "you're kidding, right?" at inappropriate times. Like, for example, the recent dinner party where I had someone quite earnestly say to me, "Some of the best moments of my life have been defined by the wine that I'm drinking." In my own ever-so-sophisticated "best moment," I practically blew my cab merlot all over the finely laid table (out my nose, of course) while sputtering in disbelief. If only I'd had a toddler in tow! I could have pointed to the little darling and said, "Oh, sorry—didn't mean to do that—it's just that Nicholas shoved a lima bean up his nose and I couldn't help myself." Instead, I said, "Some of my *worst* moments are defined by the gallons of wine I've quaffed down the night before." Yes, with toddler in tow I might have hidden my base-level behaviour from these kind folk for at least one more night.

I try not to travel solo much anymore, no matter where I go.

Tags: Kids. Handy Diversions.

August 2
We Don't Need No Stinking Rules

A Toronto-based research group recently discovered that The Chosen (i.e., BBSP owners and users) actually spend *more* time working than their prehistoric counterparts. Duh. Is this really surprising? Any BB user worth their salt knows that the beauty of the device is that it allows you to work all the time—if you want to. And that, my friends, is the key part of the phrase. *If you want to.* With a BB, you discover how much of a workaholic you really are. This is useful information. I predict that many BB-using employees will burn out quicker and resign faster as they continue to jam two years' worth of work into seven and a half months.

However, as with all annoying and ubiquitous research findings, this comes with recommendations, some of which are, well, frankly disturbing. From the inevitable "Just turn it off" (really!) to forgetting about the BB completely and actually logging "face time" (seriously, have you seen the faces on people who don't use a BB?) to (you'll love this) *apologizing* for messages coming in ("I'm sorry I'm so popular and powerful and that others want to get hold of me." Hard to make that drip with sincerity, isn't it?), we users must nip these alarming trends in the bud. I have witnessed a "No BB" sign and have heard of employers actually taking the devices away at the meeting room door! I ask you, when better to review email messages then when stuck in a *meeting*? A branch of the Canadian government has actually mandated that its employees

NOT turn on their BBSPs on weekends, in order to force said employees to re-establish some balance in their lives. Okay. First of all, hello, Big Brother. Second, the employees who want to turn off their BBs are already doing so. The ones who want to keep them on, will. They'll just take to emailing other employees who they know are also willing to break the rules by being—I don't know—dedicated to their work. And third, seriously, people, these are federal government employees. If they're anything like me, I guarantee that 50% of their emails are personal. Do the math: if they're using their BBs for personal stuff during the week when they're supposed to be working, "letting" them use it on the weekend will ensure that they're giving 100 percent—at least 100 percent of what a federal government employee is supposed to contribute (deduct 5 percent for GST, and another 40 percent just because). A dedicated employee is *not* a bad thing, and if staying in touch with the office is more pleasant than facing one's personal life, surely that counts as a kind of stress reliever. And that's good, right?

It has to be. I think that reviewing emails while standing in line has actually eradicated the "line rage" that used to result from the frustration of wasting time. Now when you're stuck behind that loser with his 17 different types of lottery picks, you can effectively utilize your time and be more productive. Or at least achieve that next level on BrickBreaker. You're in line at a government office anyway. It's all good.

Tags: Federal Government. Scary.

August 11
"The Rules," BlackBerry Smartphone Style

I was in a movie lineup with my kids today—the perfect place to pull out Seamus and catch up on some email gossip, surf the Net for a new chicken recipe—hell, even play a round or two of BrickBreaker. So I failed to notice when we all moved two steps forward. Only for a nanosecond, though, as of course my kids pushed me forward (they're now well trained to react to my BB moments, and they didn't have popcorn in their hot little hands yet). But this nanosecond was apparently enough of a time lapse and disturbance to the Mom behind me who screeched, "Hey, get your head out of your BB and pay attention to your children!" Are you serious? Pay attention to my children doing what, picking the brown sticky stuff off their pants and smelling it? What is with this growing anti-BB movement? I'm a Rules Girl, and I've come up with a few rules that users might want to start spreading into society at large. Before long, these rules will seem like they've always been there—just like the rule that says it's socially acceptable to eat asparagus and bacon with your fingers (I know!).

Rule 1: It is perfectly acceptable to start all conversations/parties/meetings/home births, etc., with "Sorry, I might have to answer this. Work, kids, you know." Rule applies even if those kids are toddlers, away at college, or on a trip around Europe with their sensible grandparents—or if you are an art history professor.

Rule 2: BB users have reserved access to the back row in movie theatres. This allows us to check any incoming messages without being told to turn off that (allegedly) annoying glowing screen. We'll be able to catch up on the plot of *Beverly Hills Chihuahua* when we're done, don't worry.

Rule 3: Should you forget to respond to someone the first time they say "I love you," you are allowed a BBSP "mulligan."

Rule 4: The yelling of "Hey, CrackBerry whore" at people engrossed in messages far more interesting than the goofs in front of them is (like farting on an elevator) simply not allowed. The fact that some secretly take this as a compliment in no way affects the rule.

Rule 5: The phrase, "Wow, you buzz a lot" is an acceptable pickup line in any bar. Particularly those frequented by brokers or journalists. Same goes for "Is that a BB in your pocket or are you just happy to see me?"

Perhaps if more of us were engaged in sending and receiving emails than in the pursuit of sex and procreation we could substitute one orgasmic experience for another and make the world a better place. Or at least a quieter one. You with me on this movement? Pick up a BB and put down that Barry White CD. The euphoria of the BB buzz ... don't underestimate it.

Tags: CrackBerry Whore. Whatever.

August 20
Things You Might Not Know About BrickBreaker

After hours of selfless and time-consuming "research," I have discovered that BrickBreaker is not a good game. It's really not. Really really not. It's similar to Pong, which some of us experienced as our first introduction to TV/video games. Remember? A big white bar simply bounced a big squarish ball across the screen to another big white bar. If you wanted to get really fancy you could flip the switch to "hockey," which would provide you with "defensive" white bars as well. The controls were so stiff—mine actually had dials—they make a Wii Workout pale in comparison. Sure, BrickBreaker has a few more options than Pong, but the utility of most of these is lost on me. So, after months of playing, I still have the following questions/concerns. Can anyone help?

• What actually causes a bubble to drop from a brick? A direct hit from a laser can do it, and so can a hit of the ball, but a bomb or gun shot cannot. Why?

• What is the use of the bomb? It shakes up the screen and is just plain annoying. Yes, I know it gets rid of a whole brick at once but I don't think it's worth the flashing ball and the aggravation.

• What's with the lasers? They are seriously the weakest ever invented. Two shots to eliminate one broken-down brick? Honestly. They're more like a ray of sunlight captured with a magnifying glass and directed to one targeted spot. The bricks don't even really break, either, they just sort of melt a bit. Arg.

• Does anyone hate the "flip" bubble as much as I do? I think you should get extra points (or an extra life!) for hitting just one ball back when mistakenly on the flip option. Don't you?

• Why does the counter at the side count the "gun ammo?" You can't save it up from round to round, you can't add it on if you hit two gun bubbles in the same level. As far as I can tell, it's there mostly to remind you that you don't have any ammo. Yes, I've been paying attention.

• Why doesn't a bomb explode the steel grates? You'd think a bomb would explode steel grates. A *gun* does, in this game. I'm just saying.

• Am I the only one who *looooves* getting the "long" paddle? I can do anything with the long paddle—except flip. But you can't have both of those at the same time ... can you? *Ooooh.*

• Tilting the screen to get a ball to go inside the steel grate hell in level 14 does nothing. *Nothing.*

• Why isn't there an option to play with an infinite number of lives ... just to see those nirvana-type levels up above 26, 27? We just want to see what we're missing during a "real" game. There's nothing like the thrill of getting to a virgin level. Except getting seven life bubbles in, like, three levels. That is *so* cool.

• If you have a moment of wild abandon and deliberately catch the "multi" button, you will soon lose that life. You can't keep that many balls in the air and you'll lose sight of the one and only that matters. Trust me on this.

• Why can't you transfer your old BrickBreaker score over to your new BB? I had to start all over—with a stiff wheel. No fair!

I told you it's a stupid game. The most frustrating thing about it is that even if I have the sound on "mute," fellow BB users automatically know I'm playing it. I'm running the wheel back and forth like mad and typically one doesn't read emails in this fashion, unless they are of the amazing-content variety—"He said what? I have to read that again!". I'm also hitting the space bar like a maniac. (Damn lasers again. Did the inventor know the meaning of the word "laser" when he created this game?) Try to resist playing the game: not even a level a day (which I know you've done to see if attacking it fresh makes a difference) and not even in the bathroom when you don't have any new emails come in during your, um, activities. I try not to play. I try not to be caught playing. I'm weak. Someone help me.

Tags: BrickBreaker. Space/time continuum.

August 22
Mars and Venus? You Bet Your Ass.

Previous studies (likely conducted by men) have suggested that women speak many, many more words per day than men. (Perhaps the fact that we're not locked away alone on top of a toilet seat for significant periods of time has something to do with it.) But a new study has proven that the difference is "statistically insignificant." Sadly, the study didn't investigate the difference in the *value* of words spoken by men versus women. I thought I'd do my own unbiased comparison. I've been working on this for a few weeks, now, and am ready to share the results.

Scenario 1: Upon greeting long-lost friends
Women: Oh my god, it's so great to see you! You look fabulous! How are the kids?
Men: Hey. Dave, right? Did you catch the game last night? I had to turn it off.
Women: Yes, Mike is fine, the kids are great, and we've moved. The new neighbourhood is terrific and we'd love to have you come over sometime.
Men: Better go or Linda will kill me. I'm supposed to be helping out with the kid's birthday party. Don't ask me which one. See ya.

Scenario 2: During the birth of a first baby
Women: Wow, this hurts! I can't believe the pain. I'm so happy

you're here beside me and able to share this beautiful, bonding experience we will forever remember. Ouch.
Men: Suck it up.

Or something to that effect.

Perhaps the strong, silent type doesn't really exist. We need to consider this carefully. Do we want these guys to be chatty or do we want them just to be quiet sometimes? If men knew when to talk and when to shut the frig up, they could save themselves quite a bit of trouble. Times to talk include over dinner; at any major sporting event; during a long and boring car ride; outside the school classroom before an interview; and at a party when you don't know too many people besides each other. Times not to talk include any time we're on the phone; emailing; watching television; gossiping with a friend; or reading a book. Back off. Try to become a sensitive, in-tune, intuitive type of guy. We women are adaptable to change—mostly—although there are still a few things that can throw us for a loop. So shut up.

Tags: Men. Silent. Annoying.

August 28
Not Even *My* Children Are Perfect

It's been almost a week since I last updated this journal. I'm putting Seamus down now, and turning off that damn game. Shit. The kids are calling me. Hell, they can wait for a minute. No one's crying. They probably just want another juice box and I can never deal with those damn straws anyway. "Suck it out of the top, kids!"

It occurs to me (as I listen to them foraging in the kitchen) that the frustration of playing BrickBreaker might be matched only by the frustrating things our children do, and our predictable responses to those frustrating things. The definition of insanity after all, is doing the same thing over and over again and expecting a different result. Yes, that's right. It's also the definition of parenting. When a child starts crying, we say he's tired. He says he's not tired and we say that's what a tired person would say while crying. When another says she's full at the dinner table we say, "Well I guess you're too full for dessert." She says, "No, there's room for that." He wants to order something in a restaurant you *know* he either won't like or won't finish. He orders it anyway, and secretly you hope he proves you wrong. He doesn't and then he says he didn't know it would be that big or taste that bad. When you tell them to hurry up, they slow down. Your teenage daughter will beg to go clothes shopping with you so she can ignore every piece of advice you offer and every suggestion you make. You will return home with a $165 coat she will never wear (and you told her that) but you can't let her freeze, and dammit why is *your* coat always missing on the coldest days? When you tell them to be quiet they just find something new to scream about. When you tell a 5-year-old you will throw their favourite blanket out of the car window if they continue to kick the back of your seat, you never do. And they keep on kicking. They never finish a bowl of cereal, a whole sandwich (including crusts), the third piece of pizza they begged you to give them, or the second pop you ordered for them in a restaurant. They can never find their outdoor runners, their favourite winter hat, their Nintendo charger, their left dance shoe, their right glove, the little thing that digs out the wheels in their wheeling runners, the note from the teacher, the toy they borrowed from a friend that you have to return, the DVD from the rental store, or the phone numbers for the kids they were supposed to have over that afternoon until you discovered that three of them have a mysterious rash. In fact, the only thing more frustrating than all of this is that, no matter what they do, children still know how to make you melt with a well placed "I love you" and a run-and-jump hug. They know how to take their "game" to the next level.

Got to go. The teenager wants to shop.

Tags: Love as a weapon. What else is new?

September 2
Unexpected Benefits of the BlackBerry Smartphone

Wait! What's that sound? It's the sound of . . . just me tapping away on Seamus, totally uninterrupted by adolescent rants, doors slamming, drinks spilling, boogers flying, clothes ripping, and refrigerator doors being ripped off their hinges. Yes, it's the first day of school and all four of them are gone. I'm sorta high. And it's giving me some time to navel gaze about the one constant lovely thing in my life (besides the aforementioned soldiers of noise) that makes my days brighter. Yes, I know that many people who shun the BB are under the misconception that it is *only* for sending and receiving emails. In the past eight months or so I have discovered that this wonderful little device is much, much more than that. In addition to elevation of one's social and business status, a BB also comes in handy when faced with the following situations:

• Having to make conversation with boring and sanctimonious women at the school bus stop (where these two lovely personality traits can and do live together in perfect harmony). "Oh, sorry—be right with you after I answer this very important email about a very important meeting I have with some very important people about something, well, very important. You go on with your dissection of judging at the last science fair and whether offering pepperoni as the only alternative to cheese for pizza lunches is contravening human rights law."

- Spending, well, more time than I planned in the public washroom at Starbucks. A dodgy meal, a late night, one too many zombies—all of these things have landed me where I'd much rather not be. At home, there are magazines and novels to read, even a shampoo bottle in a pinch. Rinse twice. Really? Who calls that 1-800 number? But when I'm not in my own magazine or product-ridden bathroom, it can be really boring just sitting there. Now I just fire up Seamus. I have learned not to Purell the keys afterward. A few germs never hurt anyone (but, yes, reread the entry on reasons not to borrow a Black-Berry if you're concerned).

- Hiding from my children's latest request to do arts and crafts. I suck at arts and crafts, but I'm really good at Brick-Breaker. I can tell them it's work, and then make sure they can't see the screen. Let them deal with the inevitable bad cutting-and-pasting grade in junior kindergarten. Builds character.

- Avoiding commitments. Seamus allows me to perform a "faux" calendar check for social dates to which I don't want to commit. "A fundraising meeting at the school? On the 8th? Let me look that up. Oh, I've got an appointment I can't move. And I was so looking forward to the presentation by the magazine representatives on Targeting the Illiterate: Leave No Stone Unturned, and that School Gym Fan Can Be Ours!"

- Sitting alone in a bar or restaurant while my companion is a) late, or b) taking way too long in the bathroom. No trouble! I'm *somebody* because I have a BBSP to pull out. I *want* to be alone. I *meant* to be alone. (Shoot, no new messages in the past two hours.) This totally replaces the social coolness of smoking from the '80s. I think if I were to smoke and use my Black-Berry at the same time I might pass out.

These hidden benefits of BB ownership can far outweigh the "electronic leash" label this pestering device has earned.

I suppose there can also be unexpected benefits of child ownership. I'll enter my thoughts if/when they come to me.

Tags: BlackBerry benefits. Ahhhhhh.

September 15
Benefits of Child Ownership

I promised you thoughts on the benefits of child ownership. Two weeks ago. I've been thinking long and hard. Let's face it . . . not everyone loves children. I am a mother of four and I include myself in this category for not insignificant parts of the day. I get it. Kids can be a challenge like no other. But I do have a problem with those anti-child people who belong to associations that are against *anyone* having children (except for their own parents, of course). The "Childless by Choice" movement has gained some momentum in an environmentally aware society, where the footprint of each person is considered to be harmful to the planet. Overpopulation is clearly a serious issue and much damage is being done as we invent new modes of transportation and new leisure activities . . . and I won't even mention Spandex. With each successive generation, we seem to find fresh ways to pillage the planet.

But think what we'd be missing without children. Think about the toys and things that might not ever have been invented! From my own childhood, I recall "clackers" (anyone else remember these glass balls of death on a string?), the footsie (that ring you'd tie around your ankle and spastically jump over), SuperSliderSnowSkates (which were essentially like strapping a Krazy Karpet snow slider to your feet), and pet rocks (seriously)—all of which were toys adults enjoyed playing with as well. It's no secret that the gaming industry is responsible for motivating many men to tackle fatherhood, if only to have a legitimate excuse to play "Death & Dismemberment XII" and pass it off as father/son bonding time.

This phenomenon has been around since the days of Pong. It's my theory that entire industries have been working overtime to disguise the fact that the diversions they typically target to children are in reality enjoyed mostly by middle-aged men. But they don't own a Nintendo DS Lite, you say? Do an office poll and I think you'll discover that 99 percent of the men have downloaded at least one game—probably Meteor—onto their handheld devices.

Other things we wouldn't have if there weren't children?

- The ability to use the expression "na na na na boo boo."
- The mind-numbing and chillaxing (just threw that word in to see if my teenagers are still reading my blog and are adequately mortified) side effects of building a Lego tower.
- Being convinced to do a backward somersault even knowing that it could result in an unfortunate fracture, or, in extreme circumstances, dismemberment.
- The ability to justify the expense of a cleaning lady. "What, there's only two of you and you're out all day and you can't keep the house clean?" Who among us *didn't* hear that from our parents just after we "set up house." Now I frequently use the "but I have *four* kids" argument to great effect. The fact that my house is messy five minutes after the front door closes on my beleaguered cleaning goddess is beside the point.
- The perfect cover story for why you still have all of those *Archie Digest*s in your house (double issues only, please), and why a few of them happen to be on *your* bedside table. Haven't you heard of bedtime stories?
- Ready-made excuses for jam stains on the kitchen wall; pen

marks on the leather couch; mysterious and disturbing blotches on the bathroom rug; schmutz on your *own* shirt; that family-sized package of Cheese Doodles in the cupboard; cream soda in the fridge; and the world's messiest minivan. Please note: The minivan *only* comes with the children. I'm deeply concerned about the child-free people who drive them.

For those individuals who remain committed to not ruining—I mean enhancing—their lives with the addition of children, here's a suggestion to help curb the occasional urge to procreate: Get a BlackBerry smartphone. It's about as time consuming, but cheaper in the long run.

Tags: Children. Good things.

September 17
Resisting Your Inner Hockey Mom

We all know the traditional definition of "hockey mom:" red-faced yelling harridan screeching about the bad referees and coaches who don't recognize athletic brilliance, and easily identified by her padded seat cushions, hockey jackets, and ubiquitous Tim Horton's coffee cup, extra large. Most Modern Mothers will resist the stereotype with every fibre of their being. Good luck with that.

When my son started asking about hockey, I convinced him, year after year, that he needed just a few more skating lessons before he could pick up a stick. It wasn't until he found himself dressed as a Teletubbie (complete with yellow tights) in the annual skating show that he suspected we were leading him down a totally different path. My husband and I gave in and finally signed him up at age 10, a relatively geriatric age for most Canadian children—especially boys. Our tomboyish daughter jumped in at 5, and our youngest has at least one hockey camp under his belt, at the tender age of 4.

So, I often find myself at the arena, sitting on a worn wooden bench, sipping my coffee, refusing to give into any sort of raised voice or inkling of enthusiasm. I read books, played on my BB (duh! It's no mystery why the person who invented the BB was Canadian. The poor man was bored stiff at one too many hockey arenas), cleaned out my purse, and had polite conversations with the only other normal-looking women there (scarcer and scarcer as the years went on and the level got higher). Once in a while I'd find myself eking out a small "Go, Alex" or "Yes, Bridget," but for the most part I was able to resist making any derogatory remarks about the other team, the coach or referee, or any other hockey parent on a competing team. Until this afternoon. I found myself doubting the referee's calls, yelling support for calls against the other team (it is one of life's biggest mysteries how a referee can make ridiculous calls on one side, but spot-on ones for the enemy—I mean, the other little children), and feeling euphoric over the win of my son's team. But that wasn't the worst of it. I'm almost embarrassed to talk about it. After we raced home from the game and headed out to a friend's for dinner, our conversation stayed on the hockey game. It was part of the first string of words out of my mouth—*at a dinner party*. One of the other women (no kids, lucky her) said, "You're such a hockey mom, Kathy," and there was nothing I could do to counteract it. It had happened. It's a slippery slope and now I'm quite worried about attending another game. What if it gets worse?

Here's the thing: Next weekend we have our *real* challenge—the hockey tournament. Yep, staying in a crappy roadside hotel playing in a town in the middle of nowhere, in a contest where every team takes home a trophy and the majority of goals scored are still flukes, freak accidents, or OGs (own goals, for the luckily uninitiated). My husband and I are missing a neighbourhood party to get to this tournament (yup, the kids' social life has taken over ours), we're paying money to stay at the hotel (which could have gone toward a rocking pair of boots), and worst of all, we're sort of looking forward to it, as our daughter is representing the team in one of the skills competition events. I will be expected to cheer. I may do so. But I refuse to allow this enthusiasm to leave the arena. Or during, via email. I may even turn off Seamus. Desperate times and all.

Tags: Hockey Moms. Apocalypse.

September 20
Who are we, really?

Self-image has always been important for women. But in the age of categorizing mothers—the stay-at-home mom, the career mom, the supermom, the hockey mom (shut up)—we often find ourselves caring as much about who we *aren't* as we who we are. Let me explain. We don't want to be Mrs. Kravitz from *Bewitched*—a nosy, gossipy, old-fashioned stay-at-home mom with nothing to do but vacuum and complain about her neighbours. We also don't want to be that gym rat mom who spends all her time in spandex, sipping lattes and complaining about the latest reno. No real desire to be a shopping mom either, hiding away her bags of swag before poor, overstressed dad gets home. Add to all of this the fact that we also worry about our "outside" appearance—how we appear to others—and we're doomed. A good part of our outside look is determined by the amount of time we spend on what goes *in* the clothes, i.e., our bodies. In my case, this includes lovely childbearing hips and the scars of pregnancy and childbirth. Can you relate?

I was watching a *Leave it to Beaver* the other day, and besides being mystified as to how June got those boys to put on blazers and ties after announcing gleefully that they had a drop-in afternoon guest, I was mesmerized by something else—June's figure. Yes, I now understand how her boobs got so pointy (Madonna wore hers on the outside, which provided the "aha!" moment), but mostly I was totally jealous of her slim, fat-free figure. How did she do it? We never saw June slipping on her Lululemons and heading out the door to the gym, or even picking up a tennis racquet. The only equipment she ever had in her hand was a vacuum or a spatula. She did spend a lot of time at the kitchen sink, though, while the rest of the family ate and she delivered her famous, "Ward, we've got to do something about the Beaver" lines. Perhaps the woman never ate. It's annoying. Just like the woman who wrote the book *French Women Don't Get Fat*, another phenomenon that left me perplexed. (No, you're not mistaken. I am often mystified or perplexed.) The author not only advocates eating all the fine food and drink life has to offer, especially in France, but also claims to absolutely abhor any "scheduled" or "forced" physical activity or workout. Apparently, we're supposed to be able to maintain our shape by taking brisk 30-minute walks, jaunting down to the local market, or zipping up the stairs instead of taking the elevator. Perhaps she neglected to mention that in order to remain slim and eat anything, the stairs in question are up the southwest leg of the Eiffel Tower.

So, as many Modern Moms do, I try to get to the gym. While there, though, I'm hit by conflicting emotions as I slave away in the Body Pump weight-lifting class, listening to the machinations of the alarmingly young and firm trainer as she invokes us to "pay the rent," and "work it, work it" and "think about the body part." Should I really be "working it"? Do I *need* to think about it? Can't I just find a half-hour walk somewhere? Who exactly am I paying this rent to? I decide to go with the "brisk walk" option, North American style. I move over to the treadmill and walk at a speedy pace—okay, faster than a saunter but maybe less than a scurry—for half an hour. Hmmmm. Burned about 100 calories—not even a teaspoon of peanut butter gone there. And French people don't eat peanut butter . . . do they? So, I'm either working at it too hard, or not enough. And I still don't look like June Cleaver. Maybe she had some corset action going on there. Maybe all that work on the Beaver was burning those calories off.

There is at least some solace to be found in the fact that June Cleaver was a fictional character, albeit portrayed by a real actress (a demographic known for their practical eating and exercise habits!). It can be hard to find a good modern mom to emulate, fictional or otherwise. Do we all aspire to be like Deborah on *Everybody Loves Raymond* (even *I* think she's bossy, and I'm on *her* side most of the time), or one of those damn Desperate Housewives? Not so much.

Tags: Beaver. Snicker. Snicker.

September 25
The "Environment" and Other Annoying Diversions

Today at the school bus stop an 11-year-old spied my omnipresent BB on my belt and said "Eww. They're bad for the environment, you know." Apparently she'd heard a story about BB signals confusing honey bees and subsequently wiping out entire hives. I believe this unfounded rumour was started by her BlackBerry-opposing parents, but it made me think about how the words "bad for the environment" have come to define the worst social and political behaviour we can possibly exhibit (over, say, axe-murdering). But there seems to be an overriding position that protecting the "environment" is a relatively new proposition. Come on!

Our grandmothers and even some of our mothers used cloth diapers before they were told they "had" to. They had no alternative. Forty or 50 years on, we've been through the cycle of disposable diapers in every size and shape—and even, for a crazy moment, sex. Yes, I will admit to shopping for diapers for my newborn baby 16 years ago and honestly being upset when I discovered they were out of "girl" diapers and I was going to have to put her in "boy" ones. What a loser. Now we've come full circle, and many social and environmental activists are insisting that we should return to the cloth diaper. There are many studies that prove that, in fact, cloth diapers are not more environmentally friendly, due to the amount of water, bleach, energy, et cetera it takes to get them clean. I really don't want to delve too deeply into that debate (it is, after all, about diapers), but it does raise the whole environmental "footprint" discussion, which has been fuelled by the hot new enviro-celeb cult. From Leo DiCaprio to Al Gore and everyone in between (oh, wait, there's actually no one in between these two), public concern about the world around us has gone from being an altruistic ideal to a mandated and sanctimonious responsibility. It is the new religion, and the zealots are coming out in full force.

About two months before she adopted a bouncing baby boy, singer Sheryl Crow, in a sincere (if clearly misguided) effort to make the world a better place, announced that we should all be able to get by on one piece of toilet paper per bathroom visit—except, she generously offered, "on those pesky occasions where two or three could be required." I've never heard of a bowel movement referred to as a pesky occasion (for me, that phrase conjures up images like entertaining the in-laws for dinner, or that yearly pap smear). Hmmm. I don't know about you, but the use of toilet paper in my house—by myself, my children, and my husband—is substantially greater than one piece per visit. Not that I want to get into details, but seriously, Ms. Crow! I know you're skinny but even the tiniest ass . . . oh, never mind. I'm just glad she has a child now. That bouncing bundle of joy will give her a big fat reality check—particularly if she eschews wet wipes (which, as an environmentalist in good standing, she should) and goes the one-square route with her son. I've emptied entire tissue boxes on a three-year-old's nose, Sheryl, my friend, so good luck with that.

On a more serious note (really, work with me here), the whole "footprint" discussion does raise interesting ideas and philosophies about the impact we have on the world. Some footprints can more easily be measured (how much garbage we create, for example, or the fossil fuels we consume), but I think there are some important "hidden" footprints that need to be measured as well. These may be more like messy "fingerprints" than entire footprints, but they are still worth noting. Consider:

• the change in the atmosphere and shift in the earth's climate that occurs upon the eruption of a baby's rear end after a healthy dose of smoked fish,
• the scream a toddler lets out when you inadvertently put on her shoes before she's ready to have them put on,
• the sheer ferociousness of a teenage girl's disdainful look (brought on only by her younger brother or always annoying mother),
• the sonic boom of the preteen door slam upon discovering that 11-year-olds are apparently not allowed to have their belly buttons pierced without permission,
• the ultimate positive energy flow that emanates when a long-suffering husband realizes that yes, it is in fact his birthday, so guess what we're doing tonight, honey?

We are right to be concerned about the environment and the world we leave behind. This all, of course, confirms my support and addiction to the BB and its ability to allow us to communicate in written format without leaving a paper trail, or so I explained to my Grade 6 critic this morning. Never mind the fact that the day they invent a mini-printer for the BB will be a sad day indeed for those of us clinging to our environmental argument in support of use. Maybe I'll take to driving the kids to school and avoiding the stop altogether.

Tags: Toilet paper. Having a baby. Getting a clue.

September 30
Stay At Home, Dad

Oh my, the neighbourhood is abuzz this morning. A new family just moved in and the waves of horror started almost immediately. Really there should be a central database to track these guys—yes, that's right, I'm talking about that new threat to all caring mothers—the rare and much-maligned Stay at Home Dad, or SAHD. We just got one. He hangs out at the park. He's at the Starbucks, the swimming pool, even (gasp) the school office. Let me explain for those of you who haven't experienced this yet.

Upon spotting a SAHD, most women assume that the specimen is a) out of work, b) lazy, c) working some sort of angle, or d) the owner of a low IQ. Ironically, this sort of filter is not used on the stay-at-home-mom crowd (okay, except by me a little bit—see my previous book, *Journey to the Darkside*, for a full explanation of my skewed reasoning). There is a paradox in this. In an ideal world, one might assume that the men could be doing something "better," but they are selflessly choosing to take a secondary or "easy" road. Hahahahahaha. We so have *not* come a long way, baby.

Recent studies have shown that men are less likely to get engaged with the stay-at-home world—which is mostly made up of women—and see their time in the domestic realm as a temporary "leave" from the real world, rather than a valid career choice. Perhaps if they had some good job perks, they might find a reason to embrace this lifestyle and let go of their unfulfilled corporate dreams. In order to develop the perks, we first must look at what's important to today's modern man:

- *Title:* There's nothing like flipping out that business card at a bar or meeting to pump up a sagging male ego. If SAHD's were able to print their own cards, with a pimped-up title that included the words "strategy" or "development," they'd like that. Now if they could only find a bar that allowed strollers, or a meeting where business cards might actually be exchanged (that emergency school council gathering on the future of Cupcake Day is just not going to cut it).
- *Project list:* It's okay if the list includes items such as "remove gunky shit from stroller." As long as there are columns labelled "Project Name," "Milestones," "Next Steps," and "Responsibility," it's all good. Let him tape some large sheets of paper around the room with the headings "Parking Lot" and "New Ideas" as well.
- *Weekly update meetings:* Some coffee, an agenda, donut holes, and the opportunity to say, "I think I have the floor right now" (even if "the floor" is a small carpeted area at the indoor playground), can feel good. How's that diaper rash coming along, Judy? Last week you said you'd have closure on it.
- *Summer hours:* Every second Friday, the SAHD is allowed to crack open a beer at 2 p.m., instead of at the usual 4 p.m. Yahoo! Live it up. As long as the vacuuming is done.
- *Executive washroom:* Oh, for God's sake, they stink up that master-suite bathroom so badly that no one else would dare enter it anyway. Give them a big silver key on a horrible sports logoed keychain and they'll be happy.
- *Tickets to special events:* The "Tot 'n Toddler Fashion Show" at the mall, the "Toy Tea" at the hospital, and the "Holiday

Tupperware Event" could substitute for sports events, gala dinners, and golf days, if you print nice tickets and provide giveaways and the chance to win a t-shirt with a bank logo on it. If there's a VIP lounge, go for it.

Men's egos are different from women's. Men often need to feel as though they are winning some sort of invisible competition. The "score," so to speak, is easy to keep if you work in the corporate world and can compare the size of your cubicle to the one of the next person, or gaze adoringly down on an organizational chart that shows an ultra-impressive box with your name in it at the top of the heap. It's hard to manufacture this type of one-upmanship at home, however. So, in order to keep the SAHD satisfied and fulfilled in the kitchen and behind the grocery cart, you'll have to get creative. Make them think they are forging new territory, opening exciting business ventures, and generally doing pretty well at what they've been seeing as an easy job for all these years. Don't take it too far, however, or he'll be planning a conference in Florida with his newly hired administrative assistant.

Tags: Men. Ego. Men. Ego. Repeat as necessary.

October 2
Love 'Em, Hate 'Em

I do love to hate my BlackBerry smartphone; and I hate to love it. This is similar to how I feel about my 2-year-old, whom I adore one minute and want to send out for a DNA test the next. Don't get me wrong, I *love* the little guy but I need to get him out of my face quite often. (The fact that my current "little" guy is fourth in the family lineup has him unfairly haunted by the ghosts of toddler behaviours past; my automatic reaction to any sly grin is an immediate time out. Honestly, I know exactly where *that's* going.)

Offspring inspire strong feelings in parents across the animal kingdom. Some, in fact, like to eat their young, abandon the weak, or sacrifice a few, but for our purposes I'll deal with the more positive human parenting roles. While "bonding" can take different parents varying periods of time, generally speaking by the time the child is walking and talking there have been at least some positive feelings generated on both sides. However, these are usually counterbalanced by some fairly strong negative feelings most often generated during times of duress (i.e., those times when they are not doing exactly what you want them to do [i.e., most of the time]).

I know I am not alone in how much I love my children when they're asleep. This feeling normally takes over minutes after I find myself wanting to pass them off to gypsies (while they were actually conscious). Of course, I also love them when they're awake, but sleep provides a beneficial respite from their in-your-face-behaviour. By the way, this is sort of like when you and your BlackBerry are out of range and you can't do anything but gaze lovingly at it and wonder what terrific experiences it will bring when it jumps back to life. Over the years I have learned to be particularly wary of parents who seem to be nice to their children all the time! Even when the child in question is behaving in a manner that is, let's say, less than satisfactory (punching, kicking, smearing bodily fluids, that sort of thing). You'll hear them simper, "Oh darling, I so admire your creativity but let's try to remember that not everyone likes to have their legs drawn on with a permanent marker. I think Nicholas's Mom would prefer to see your artwork on paper." These are the folks who will rarely admit out loud that they are thrilled to bits to see the kids get on that school bus that first day in September, or be dropped off at a friend's house for an extended "playdate." What's up with that? It is simply unnatural to cherish every single moment with your child. Space is a good thing, people! Occasional separations from our children give them the chance to miss us—and vice versa. Absence not only makes the heart grow fonder, but also blurs painful memories of obstinacy, tantrums, craziness and other surly antics in which all children engage.

Just don't ask me to put Seamus away during the day. He's cuter awake.

Tags: Sleep. Precious. Fantasy.

October 10
I've Got News for You, Unconverted . . .

I may have made a slight mistake in my parenting today. As the children yammered on about their scintillating school-day escapades, my daughter caught me looking at my BB and screamed down the street, "You love your BB more than you love me! I'm going to throw it down the sewer!" I'm fairly certain that only the adjacent four houses or so heard me reply, "You do, and you'll never see that special blanket of yours again, sister."

As a frequent BB user (if your definition of "frequent" is "constant"), I am often accused by children, husband, friends, and passing acquaintances of not paying attention to them while I am sending or receiving messages. (In the case of BB messages, by the way, it is far more satisfying to receive than to send.) I always reassure them, in turn, that I am indeed enraptured by their Grade 2 math, the exciting description of the banking services employee offer "fiasco," or the latest and greatest accomplishment of their natural-athlete son. As a woman, I can usually dredge up some part of the conversation and spew it back. This suggests to my human friends that I *do* listen to them and that I'm not held slave to my electronic buddy. But here's the thing: I'm lying. I'm not paying attention and, yes, whoever is on the other end of the electronic message *is* more interesting than you are. Man! It feels good to have that off my chest.

Moms have long been able to multi-task. While speaking to

each other we can simultaneously track children, point fingers, shake our heads no, and suddenly dart across an indoor playground to catch a falling toddler—not once breaking off our answer to the last query about our holiday plans. We can do this mom-to-mom, and I think we can also do it BB-to-BB. It's totally acceptable for two card-carrying BB users to check and send messages while in the midst of a verbal conversation (playing BrickBreaker . . . not so much). But when we're around those other sorry folks (the ones without technology or toddlers), apparently we are supposed to be "engaged."

I actually think that the BB is quite advantageous for men. They are usually not listening, and this device gives their listeners a visual clue (and the men an excuse): they are in fact not listening, and haven't been for some time. In the case of most husbands, they likely haven't been listening since the days before you first slept together. For women, who are supposed to be active listeners (I'm not—I'm actually reloading when other people are speaking), this divided-attention thing is considered rude. Even though my children long ago figured out that when I'm nodding and saying "oh, okay" over and over again, I'm not really listening, nothing infuriates them more than when I'm glancing at the BBSP while they're trying to grab a minute of my so-called valuable time. This is also true of non-BB carrying spouses, who insist on your full attention at the most inopportune times. For instance, anytime a new message has buzzed into your box. "Yes, I heard what you said about your Grandmother. Her hip? How horrible."

At the risk of having this backfire horribly, perhaps what is required are some attention-grabbing phrases that the non-user can insert into the conversation. These might just get their BB buddies to look up from the screen:

- (The obvious) "Did you see the announcement on the new smartphone that's coming out? It looks really different from yours."
- "What's that stuck to the back of your BB?"
- "So, anyway, honey, I told my boss she could shove the job and figured we'd all move to the country, far away from any technology connectivity."
- "Watch out! The sprinkler is about to hit you!"
- "Mom, I need to ask you some questions about birth control before Friday night."

Failing the above, the most reasonable thing for a non-BB user to do is to walk over to the nearest computer with Internet access, sign into their Hotmail account (I *know* there is a correlation between people who still have only a Hotmail account and people who don't own a BB) and send the offending, ignoring BlackBerryer a note. It's kind of like the old days in the office when we used to phone the person sitting one cubicle over. We've just all gotten a little bit closer.

Tags: Hey, Luddites!

October 12
Thank You, Thank You, Thank You

Thanksgiving (in Canada, anyway; those of you south of the border have to wait another six weeks for your turkey). A time for reflecting on those things for which we are truly thankful, gathering together with our families, sharing cherished memories, and creating precious new ones. Oh, who am I kidding? It's a time for recrimination, backhanded compliments, outright insults, and the resurgence of long-simmering arguments. What else is family for? If they don't tell you where you're going wrong, who will? The turkey and the continually filled wine glasses are what keep most of us happy—that, and now of course, our new best friend. The BB truly is a welcome addition to any family gathering, and Thanksgiving is no exception. In fact, I found myself developing extreme gratitude for my handy sidekick during the following exchanges over stuffing and yams:

• "Hang on, Uncle Greg. I'll just Google that for you. I'm pretty sure 'real' cooks don't put tapioca in broccoli and cheese, like you're saying I should have. Here!" Recipes.com rules!
• "I really don't think this is a discussion we should have in front of the children. I don't want to be the one to explain what the phrase 'bastard cousin' means. Bridget, honey, here. Take my BB and go and play BrickBreaker or something."
• "Yes, I'm sending an email to myself right now, Mom, to remind me to call the hotel where the daughter of the friend of

your cousin Larry is staying. I'm sure she'll be thrilled to hear from me."

• "Yeah, honey, so the deep-fried turkey turned out to be sort of the disaster all those videos on YouTube woulda had us believe, eh? I'll call Pizza Pizza on my BB and we'll be eating shortly, folks. Yes, I know the number—it's on speed dial. Don't start, Mom."

• I ate so much dinner that my plastic BlackBerry holster pinged off my shiny belt and whacked my least favourite brother right in the face. Score!

Yes, Seamus has provided me with a few lifesavers—not the least of which was the call my son made from the hockey arena letting me know his ride had fallen through. Hang on, son! I'll be right there!

Tags: Turkey. Tofurkey. Fofanna. Banana.

October 20
Method to My Madness

My kids annoy me sometimes. No shit. From the moment they are born, babies can be a real pain. Through toddlerhood, grade school and the charming teenage years, children find countless ways to push the parental buttons. And even though I know I am repeating the behavioural patterns laid down by generations of weary parents before me, this button pushing can still get me wound up to the Mommy-Dearest level. The trick I've learned is to make sure that my madness, translated into the associated planning of revenge and punishment, benefits me first, and punishes *them* second. Let me provide you with an easy to understand illustration of this fine parenting technique. The other day I received a call from my teenage son, who was in the school's office:

> "Mom, you know that health form I need for my Quebec City trip?"
> "No."
> "That's because I didn't give it to you. But it's due today or I can't go on the trip. Can you come to the office and sign it for me?"

Later, my husband said to me, "Well, you didn't go, did you? He's got to learn some responsibility!" And I'll admit my immediate reaction *was* to teach him a lesson by *not* coming to the school and filling it out, and have him miss out on the school trip as a result. But hang on a minute. This trip takes him out of my house for four whole days (leaving me with only three children to harangue). Who would really feel the pain over his not going? Yours truly. You can still see the burning rubber marks on our little side street. So yes, I hastened to the school. And made him empty the dishwasher when he got home.

I tried to share this redirection of "being mad" into personal benefit with my husband the other day. This conversation took place after he complained about the same child not making it home in time to babysit his younger siblings, which caused my husband to be dangerously late for an event. In typical male fashion, instead of picking up the phone and calling the one or two friends our son might be with, he just stewed while waiting for the kid to show up and receive his punishment. Again, who's really feeling the pain here? It's satisfying to get a good mad on, but in the end, don't we all want to work toward victory for our side? Strategic warfare is something I know my husband can really get his head around. I can always get him to listen to me by threatening to cancel his History Channel subscription. If the dishwasher's empty, then put 'em to work on the laundry. Use your imagination, big boy.

I do believe this whole concept is hard for men; they prefer to see punishment as an equation of action equals reaction. That makes sense to them. But as all mothers know, common sense often goes out of the window when you're dealing with children (just ask those freaks who sleep in their cars overnight to get their kid into the "right" swimming lesson). Redirecting mad moments into scenarios where we benefit can be easy and fun. Try not to let the fact that the children are oblivious to your system and sometimes don't feel the punishment adequately enough deter you in any way. Consider:

- He will only wear one pair of jeans . . . for three weeks straight. And our issue with this is—what? Less laundry? Lower clothing bills? Honestly, if they're a little stinky, are you the one he is hanging out with all day long? Not if they're teenagers. They wouldn't be seen dead with you and now the feeling is mutual. Score.
- She eats all the "good fruit" in the house. You know, the berries. Kids can't resist them, so for some reason, we buy them only as a treat. Then we get mad if she eats them all for a snack instead of for dessert. Really people, we're only talking about a difference in timing here. Let her get away with it.
- He won't put a sweater on when it's slightly chilly. Let's review the possible consequences: There is zero probability of him getting frostbite (it's an April evening). He will get cold and a) learn a lesson, b) recognize how right Mom is all the time, and c) provide one less article of clothing to be washed, by you, tomorrow. All good.
- You won't allow her to have friends over because she is being punished. Wrong wrong wrong. Have the friends over, get her out of your hair, pour yourself a glass of wine and punish her by making her something healthy for dinner or having her vacuum the basement. Passive-aggressiveness is a fantastic parenting strategy.
- You insist on engaging in arguments with your children. Don't do it. You're just going to get mad and possibly indulge in some binge eating. Just remember that *you* always win the argument, if you want to. *You* are the boss, *they* are the peons. Tell them at the beginning of the argument that you plan on

winning, but that they are more than welcome to present their case. Makes them crazy. Just like they make you. One for the good guys.

The most important thing to remember is that *you* have to feel good about the situation. Think it through to the end. No, you really don't want them to do some annoying arts and crafts and scatter the crayons and paper all over the kitchen table. You know you'll have to clean up the mess when they move on after 7 1/2 minutes. But 7 1/2 minutes is more than enough time to crack open that chilled chard, or that cold brewski. You still win, my friend.

Tags: Crime and Punishment. Men. Sheesh.

October 26
How Can I Miss You If You Never Go Away?

I have discovered, contrary to my own core beliefs, that there are situations in which children are quite handy to own; for example, as a tool for extricating myself from unfortunate situations. It occurred to me this week that it would have been great to have had a child (or two) at my side on several different occasions. For example:

• At bus stops. After the older children have gotten on board, I am often forced to listen to an inane conversation about the pizza lunch/volunteer ratio. A little boy holding his penis and yelling "Now, Mommy, now!" would have been a fantastic excuse to back away from the scene.

• At dinner parties. My husband and I were once invited to an adults-only dinner party. Looking forward to this rare treat, I took the trouble to book a babysitter. When we arrived at the party, however, we discovered the host's maniacal band of thugs (all under the age of 5) had been invited to stay with the grown-ups for the entire evening! I was left suffering with someone else's children! If my own children had been present, I could have taken the opportunity to discipline them and escape for a few precious moments of quiet. An early escape route could also have been manufactured by pushing my prodigy to pound one of the hosts'.

• Family gatherings. Normally at these functions, one is expected to help cook or clean for the 27 guests. "But I have to take Bridget to the bathroom. Again. Yes I know she's 8. It's our special time. Here, fill my glass first."

• In lines. More times than I can count, I find myself standing in lines wondering why a) the service is so slow or b) that idiot/bitch just cut in front of me. With a child in hand as a convenient foil, I get to demonstrate my fantastic passive-aggressive skills. "No, honey I don't know why it takes 15 minutes to make another batch of fries," or "Yes, I know we're supposed to wait our turn. That lady must need to eat more than us to keep those size 16 pants up." Note: If the child in question is under the age of 2 1/2, this tactic may be unsafe.

• During flatulence episodes: I really shouldn't have had that second bean-filled burrito for lunch and now someone's made me laugh in a quiet library/store/waiting room. "Nicholas! Mommy told you that wasn't polite to do in public. Not another word about it!"

• For wardrobe mishaps: Children can provide a handy explanation for the stains on my white blouse. "Red wine? No! This is from the homemade strawberry jam I was feeding my precious this morning. I'm not the kind of mother to worry more about my clothes than their happiness."

Come to think of it, being without my children or Seamus can leave me feeling empty, baseless, and well, let's face it, free. But as with most good things in life (i.e., minced garlic in a jar, precooked bacon, and wine in a box) once experienced, there is no turning back. Both my children and my BB are integral parts of my life.

Tags: Kids. Handy. Diversions.

October 31
Trick or Treat?

Much as I've tried, I simply can't get the Barbie evening gowns to sit just right on Seamus. So I've decided it could go out dressed as:

- an 80s calculator,
- a big-ass pedometer,
- those thingies they used on *Star Trek* that require you to yell "Beam me up Scotty!"
- the "Danny Devito" remote television control model.

My biggest decision, however, is that I shouldn't start drinking wine as my own "treat" when I'm making up the bags to give out to the kids. How come no one's rung my doorbell yet?

Tags: Halloween. Sober. Scary.

November 3
Relax, Honey

Great news! I've been planning a Girls' Weekend away with some friends. Bad news. We've been planning it for 5 1/2 years. Sure, one of the great things about being a mom in this day and age is that air travel has become cheaper and easier and more accepted for short sojourns. Additionally, the advent of these alleged "Girls' Weekends" has been one of the greatest advancements in the women's movement since, well, the women's movement. Travel agencies often recommend "getting away from it all" with your spouse. While this *can* be a good thing, sometimes the hubby is a big part of the "it all" you're trying to get away from in the first place. I would venture to say that in the pecking order of holidays, getting away by yourself tops even getting away with the girls. There's less chance of a hangover, a drunken confessions, a catfight, or resentment.

The hardest part about getting away for a weekend with the girls is not convincing my husband that I'm going to do it (what, he's listening?). He's fine with that. The trick is recognizing that the real work begins once the travel arrangements have been made. For example, I am somehow solely responsible for arranging babysitters for those moments when my husband can't be with the children (even though I won't be there) and for making arrangements for pickups and drop-offs if the logistics don't work under the one-parent scheme. And I always have to prepare "the list."

I've prepared basic husband-lists that simply list what time the kids have to go to school, doctor's numbers, sports schedules, medications to be taken, even directions to the nearest grocery store (it's that big cement building with the giant red "D" on the front). I like the basic list, because it leaves off the many things I would rather my husband discover for himself (because I'm mean). For instance:

- Yes, you have to wake up the teenagers at 7:15 a.m. What you don't know is that this seemingly simple activity will take approximately 10 minutes out of your morning. Yell at them once, then twice, then nag them about packing up their knapsack before they come downstairs, then nag them about teeth brushing and combing hair. Yes, these are all things they should know, but no, they don't.
- If you find a quiet moment to read the newspaper, do it! Because sometime in the next five minutes you will have something at a critical cooking point on the stove at the same exact moment that a bum needs to be wiped, a cut needs to bandaged, and a fight needs to be broken up. Carpe diem? More like Carpe momento!
- If you yell at the children, make sure you close the windows first, particularly the living room ones that face out to the sidewalk where every one of our nosy neighbours will walk by and judge you.
- If something in the fridge stinks, throw it out. Don't ask questions.
- If a kid stinks, wash it. Don't ask questions.
- The 4-year-old cannot turn corners on his bike without running into inanimate objects. Wear runners to follow him.
- Yes, I know about the ink on the leather couch. Find your happy place.

- If the kids tell you they don't have any homework, they are either full of shit, totally clueless, or not listening. Follow up. Go into the knapsack if you have to. Wear gloves.
- Don't believe the kids when they tell you I let them eat snacks right until dinner time. Except if you're on a conference call and you need them to shut up. I've done that. Upside of this is that you don't have to make dinner as soon as you hang up.
- If a neighbour asks you to take their children for an hour or two, do it, but not without securing a return arrangement (in writing if it's that cow at number 47). Even if the kids don't want to go, send them. Not your problem.
- The grocery store gets upset if you try to put 16 items through on the 15 or less lane. Actually, I'll correct that: the grocery store doesn't care, but those seven crabby women behind you do. Take cover.

Perhaps the most important thing for my husband to remember is that when I finally arrive back home on the doorstep, he must tread very carefully. If he's done a really terrible job (e.g., curtains are ablaze, children are naked and dirty, and there are empty beer bottles on the front lawn), he'll get tonnes of grief from me about not being able to take care of his own kids. If he's done a fantastic job (house is gleaming, children are beaming and well dressed, and dinner is bubbling on the stove), I'll hate him for making it look easy. If he's smart, he'll make sure he messes up on one or two things (while being careful to have the right number of children as a baseline). Maybe I'll have missed him enough to whisper those much coveted words in his ear: "Honey, do you want me to make you a sandwich?"

Tags: A Real Getaway. Get away.

November 9
CelebuMoms and Their CelebuSpawns

When I wrote my first two books, *The Secret Life of Supermom*, and *Journey to the Darkside: Supermom Goes Home*, I took the opportunity to criticize what I like to call the "Celebrity Uber-Mom" crowd. Without a doubt, these small rants were the most popular bits with the media, and with other moms. For the media side, it's a given. Even mentioning a celebrity mom like Angelina or Madonna can guarantee a good sound bite. For the other moms, I think the popularity of these bits stemmed from that lovely tradition of building someone up just to tear them down. We do it with our friends and our family (remember when your kids used to worship you—and then they turned 9?) and we looooove to do it with those who are thinner, richer, prettier, and have better hair. We hope that the children of these women will turn out bad, because it just wouldn't be fair for these moms to be out exercising, getting their hair done, partying, showing up at premieres (i.e., having a life), *and* having their children turn out normal.

Recently, I've noticed a bit of a Hollywood formula for getting pregnant, having children, and raising them all proper-like. It goes something like this:

- Either have a child before you turn 25 (Britney) or state at the age of 40 that you're thinking about starting a family (Halle).
- Adopt a child from a third-world country to show how giving and caring you are (Madonna, Angelina).

- Don't do anything as pedestrian as dipping into the same gene pool for a second child (Christie Brinkley, Madonna, Heidi Klum)
- Make sure you choose a really weird name. Otherwise, the kid won't have enough hang-ups (Gwyneth Paltrow, Demi Moore).
- If this kid is a boy, don't cut his hair (Kate Hudson, Celine Dion).

Speaking of Hollywood, the Cannes Film Festival is upon us again. Somewhere between the red carpet and the after-party, Angelina Jolie (god love her for the endless material she provides), announced that she will be "taking a break" and spending some time at home with her *six* children. Now, say what you will about our Angelina—she steals husbands, plays with knives, wears blood vials around her neck—but I've always kind of thought she was, well, smart. She doesn't seem to display any idiotic tendencies like Britney or Michael Jackson or other nightmare celebrity parents. In her own weird way, she sort of seems to have it all together. Men dig her because they're a little bit afraid of what she might do to them. I get that. That's cool. But this idea that she's going to take some time off—a "sabbatical," I believe she called it—to spend time with her children is somewhat perplexing. Let's review: she jets around the world (flying her own planes, thank you, sister); gets fawned over by film people; has fabulous hair, makeup and wardrobe people on standby; attends premiere parties; and goes home to Mr. Pitt. Seriously. The woman believes she needs a break from *this*?

I suspect she's not going to go home and really take care of those kids, at least not in the same way most of us do (you know, the butt wiping and car seat jamming and booger scraping and all that), but why on earth would she want to give up her lifestyle to even pretend to go home and hang with the children? Is she not worried that Brad will start to lose interest? Has the woman no fear? Does she remember how she met him in the first place? I know I morphed into a much more boring person when I didn't have something like "real work" to distract me during the day. When I was gainfully employed, I didn't need to talk about diaper changes, spilled fluids (bodily and otherwise), or fights with the gossiping neighbourhood moms. I had the at-work assholes to complain about. I had some drama (if finding out that a reorganization is coming down the pipe is exciting to you); I had some romance (if the guy who grabbed my ass in the coffee line counts); and I even had comedic situations to relay (me, trying to get into that skirt from last summer). Angelina will soon discover that talking about the kids with, I don't know, *the world's sexiest man*, may soon have him looking out the window for the next lucky contestant. Call *me* crazy, but I think *she'd* better go back to being crazy before this whole mom scene blows up in her pouty-lipped face.

Tags: Brad Pitt. Sigh.

November 11
Another World . . .

Talking about Angelina the other day got me stuck on the celebrity-mom thing. That, and standing in line at the grocery store and reading all about their perfect lives as my two rapscallions hit each other over the head with a box of Cocoa Puffs. But are celebrities' lives really perfect?

Modern Celebrity Moms shoulder the burden of having the whole world watch their mistakes and critique their questionable parenting decisions. Most of us normal moms just have the in-laws to contend with. Okay, leaving the house in a teeny little skirt and no underwear is a little beyond the pale where matters of taste are concerned, but when Britney does it, we cast aspersions on her skills as a mother as well. A word of caution for those of us trying to find our inner "hot mama" while maintaining the outward appearance of raising semi-normal kids: it's easy to tip too far one way or the other and become a Skanky Mommy, or alternatively, a Mumsy Mommy.

A general rule of thumb to keep you out of the Skanky Mommy pool? Try to have fewer husbands than children. Angelina is 3 for 6 (oh, come on, she and Brad aren't married but he's whipped enough to count); Britney is 2 for 2; and Scary Spice is, well, 1 for 2 (and the second comes with a denial and a potential lawsuit—nice).

All kidding aside (yeah, right) you have to feel sorry for today's Celebrity Mom. She must appear to be a loving, supportive mother for her soon-to-be-in-therapy-or-rehab children, all while working to keep her celebrity status intact. On the surface, it would appear that women like Julianne Moore, Cate Blanchett, Julia Roberts, and even that annoying Catherine Zeta-Jones have found a nice work-life balance, while staying mostly married to the same guy (or at least only changing out every five years or so). Are they good role models? Do we *need* role models in the media? As I've always said, my life (or body) didn't resemble theirs before I had children, so why is it that I compare myself to them now? Does being a mom bond us in ways we never would have hoped for or imagined? Come on, people! Sometimes it just makes me want to take my underwear off and stagger out of a low-slung vehicle.

And the fun these ladies supply just never stops! Apparently Gwyneth Paltrow believes she has spent three years of her life "just being a housewife" and is now glad to get back out and "work." Okay, for starters, I have to imagine that the world of Gwyneth the housewife is not the same as, say, the world of Kathy the housewife. For example, I doubt Gwyneth has ever staggered through Walmart, Apple shrieking beside her for some crappy toy while baby Moses manages to simultaneously spit up, sneeze, and eject a messy poo into his stained and cracked car seat. That was me, except for the fancy baby names. Gwyneth's days were likely spent in an off-white living room, where she sipped green tea, talked on her cellphone, booked another strange meditative or colonic treatment, and tried to decide which shoulder her hair should gently cascade over. Oh, and instead of cursing out Chris Martin for once again not getting the cereal bowl into the dishwasher, or for leaving the toilet seat up, she was no doubt thinking of the 10 ways their marriage is still perfect, for that next "typical housewife" interview with a major American fashion magazine.

One thing I do have in common with celebrity moms is my attachment to my BB. You have to wonder, though (or at least I do), who is it that Lindsay Lohan, Paris Hilton, and Britney Spears could possibly be emailing? Do these girls even know how to type? I have my doubts, yet we see them in all their photo-op moments, one hand wrapped around a "coffee" and the other around a handheld device. (One has to assume that the electronic monitoring bracelet issued by the state penitentiary doesn't actually use the same frequency as the BB. Otherwise, both devices might be rendered useless for this particular market.)

As we all know, the BB *can* be annoying. When the user is engaged in a conversation and can't stop sneaking a peek, the person to whom they are speaking always feels the same way you do when you're at a party and your companion is constantly looking over your head for someone "better" to talk to. Or what about that store clerk who picks up the phone when you're standing right in front of them. My point is—stay with me—when we see Brad Pitt emailing someone with one hand, while his other arm is wrapped around Angelina Jolie, we've got to ask: Who the hell is he talking to that he's decided is more important? Isn't he already standing beside one of the "beautiful people?" Why does he need more? It's just greed, I say. Greed.

Tags: Envy. Jealousy. Fantasy.

November 15
In Case of Emergency . . .

It's my considered opinion that parents experience as many moments of sheer terror as they do of pure joy. Think about the range of feelings you experience as you race through the grocery store, checking aisle upon aisle for that scruffy little head . . . and finding it kneeling in front of a candy display. As a Modern Mom now fully in love with her BB—it's been almost a year, people! I can't remember life before it!—I now have an added layer of terror with which to contend. The BlackBerry shut down. While the fine folks at RIM mostly manage to keep us running, day and night, 24/7, we are occasionally faced with this horrific scenario. And unlike our corporate counterparts, moms can't simply start listening at the meetings, reading the paper on the commuter train, or doing some actual work while we anxiously await the restart. Everything else we do is infinitely more boring than the chance that our BBSP will start up in a second. So, we wait. And wait.

What's a Modern Mom to do while waiting? Lucky for you, I've made a list. Cut it out, put it in your wallet, and refer to it in times of emergency.

How to pretend to have a life without your BB:
1.   Do things you couldn't do with your BB in tow even if it were working—for example, anything aquatic, freezing, or boiling.
2.   Actually listen to your children while their lips are moving

and sounds are coming out—just be careful not to listen for very long as a) they will get used to it, and b) there are some things you just don't want to know.

3.   Book a romantic lunch or dinner with your partner (this works especially well if he doesn't own a BB or listen to the news, i.e., if he lives under a rock). Make the grand gesture of leaving the BB at home, or less drastically, demonstrate that you're turning it off before you have that first cocktail. (Note: The fact that you are with someone who does not own a BB is a little disturbing, but perhaps they are quite cute. Whatever works for you.)

4.   Call an elderly relative or long-winded friend whom you normally struggle to get out of speaking with. Give him or her the chance to ramble, knowing that—for once—you are not actually missing something more important.

5.   Go the movies, the opera, the theatre, the symphony, the ballet—those despised dens of "no cellphones allowed." You'll get to sit through an entire event without once faking a bathroom visit just to check your messages.

It's not easy to find a life without your BB once you've been drawn into its world. Escapism is one of my favourite parenting techniques, and my own BB experiences have allowed me to fall deeply, madly, and passionately in love with this technology, which allows me to keep one foot firmly in the land of "those who have a life/friends/worldly interests" while dealing simultaneously with the minutia of domestic life with children.

RIM reports that its biggest growth market at the moment is the consumer market. Given that the business market is completely saturated, this is not a total surprise. I'd be willing to bet a weekend with my teenage son (any takers?) that it's

Modern Moms who are leading the pack. So fall in step ladies, and join me as we continue our adventures in Modern Motherhood.

Tags: It's not over yet.

November 22
Oh, It's Wearing, Alright.

It used to be adorable when my son would say "Carry! Carry!" and I would reach down and he would wrap his skinny little arms around my neck and I would hold him close and we'd snuggle and bond. And then, the other day, the same kid, now about 20 pounds heavier, launched himself from the top stair and just about slammed me back on to the ground. There is a time and a place when carrying your children just gets illogical and impractical. And ridiculous. Or so I thought. Just when you think you've mastered another parenting tip, along comes a new trend: "baby wearing." And, no, we're not talking about the baby schmutz *all* new moms wear when they're carrying their babies around. We're talking about wearing the *baby itself.*

This has gone way beyond carrying, people. And beyond the stage of "babies." Real zealots recommend carrying the child well past what anyone could consider to be a "baby" age. When the kid hits 35 pounds at about age 2 (about the same time when stair-leaping becomes appealing, trust me), apparently you're supposed to flip them from the front carriers to a babywearing backpack. Motherhood, thy name is sherpa? So it wasn't enough they took over the inside of our bodies for more than nine months? Now we have to have them literally hanging off us for another two years? This baby accessory, along with many others, belongs in the category "for people who have no lives," which is cross-pollinated with the "for people who believe any parenting device or theory developed after 1950 is bad" category. The babywearers believe they are emulating primitive cultures in which babies are strapped to their mothers as soon as they find their way out. Hmmm ... forgive me if I'm stereotyping, but that primitive culture might also have included punching holes through lips with bones, female vaginal mutilation and, oh, I don't know, maybe some leech-driven blood-letting? Yet we're supposed to take one aspect of that lifestyle and expect it to improve the life of a perfectly normal (except for the unfortunate thing about their parents) North American child, being raised in a North American house? I'm only going to say this once (in this entry anyway): We should all have time away from our children. We should. It's not normal for them or for us to be permanently attached physically and emotionally. I worry that these children will grow up to be 45-year-old web surfers living in the basement. All the best psychos blame their abhorrent behaviour on their mothers. I want to hedge my bets and at worst be blamed for being a distant mother. If Joan Crawford had signed on to do more overseas movies, she wouldn't have had so many hanger-worthy moments.

But back to the babywearing (I haven't quite finished pillorying that particular trend). When is this 2-year-old going to learn to walk? Is he wearing a diaper back there? How do you go about replacing the hair that he is sure to rip out of your head on a regular basis? Doesn't your back hurt? How do you keep a clean body line with a toddler strapped to your back? Linen blouses? Muddy boots? These are real concerns obviously not being addressed by the babywearers. Perhaps it's just part of a secret movement looking for a subversive way to extend the already too long Canadian maternity leave from one year to two. "Look, little Bobby still needs me to carry him around. How can I possibly go back to work now? Besides, kindergarten's just around the corner."

I have now without a doubt established why I really need that RIM endorsement. The baby-product market is clearly not going to be knocking on my door anytime soon. At least the stupid-baby-product market.

Tags: Joan Crawford. Role Model.

November 30
You Have a Role to Play. Trust Me.

Here's a shocker: Parents tend to overprotect their kids. Duh! I find this to be particularly true in the school setting, where parents of tweens and even teenagers sometimes still believe their children want and need them along on a school trip, be it day or overnight. Weren't they ever 13? The last thing a child wants at this age is to be reminded that he or she even *has* a parent. It may be because the inherent existence of the parental units proves that old people (like us) have had sex, or it may just be that they think we're total dorks. And we are; compared to them and their ultra-cool teenage ways. When I helpfully point out that skateboarding god Tony Hawke is a mere few years younger than I, and a father to young children, I receive in return a look of pity. It's a look that says I do not know how uncool I am if I think I'm in the same league as Mr. Hawke. Here's some advice: Forget intellectual or philanthropic pursuits as ways to impress your young teens, and don't pick up a skateboard either. Just slide quietly and slowly into the background while keeping a hand out. You'll need it to take in dirty clothes, and notes from school, while also doling out money, clean laundry, and, eventually, car keys.

Since time began, parents have been treated as nothing more than accessories by their children, no matter what the media might have to say about the latest Hollywood trend that holds having a child on the same level as getting a much coveted Birkin bag. In fact, they may even make child-sized

Birkins. Why not? A well-known upscale retailer in Toronto recently introduced a kids' boutique that included a $245 Juicy Couture track suit. The same media that splashes pictures of Angelina, Reese, Jerry Seinfeld, and others with their fashionable young babies in their fashionable strollers in their fashionable clothes, also complains that this "narcissism-fuelled parental consumerism" has children being treated as accessories instead of people. What they perhaps don't realize is that a child may act as a "cool" or "haute" accessory for a five-second pose at a kiddie catwalk, but in real life (one that does not include a catwalk), parents more often than not find themselves to be the accessories for the children. Yes, parents are used, abused, and mistreated worse than Naomi's personal assistant. Consider these roles, any number of which you might have taken on:

- *Snack camel:* Go to any playground or soccer field, take a walk around the block, or even make that weekly trip to the grocery store and you'll hear "Mom! Where's my snack?" The dutiful parent will obligingly pull out a granola bar and juice box stored for this very purpose. There is no frickin' way my mother would ever have done that.
- *Cash dispenser:* Children point at things they want—it's a time-honoured tradition. "Mom, can I have two 25 cents?" or "But I *need* another SpongeBob baseball cap!" Because we know we need them to *shut up*, we will eventually give in.
- *Undercover agent:* Or should that be "underwear" agent? Any parent of a child aged 4 or under routinely carries around an extra pair of gitch, which they are expected to whip out at a moment's notice when, ahem, adjustments must be made. Yes, you have become a person who carries around clean underwear

for somebody else. And worse, you carry home the dirty ones.

- *Easy target:* Mostly used by the tween/teen crowd in order to elevate one's own "coolness" level by pointing out the nerdiness of a nearby parent, e.g., "His Dad wears socks with his sandals!" And kids are not even one bit concerned about lowering their voices to protect your feelings. The louder, the better.
- *Backpack mule:* School trips, picnics, park visits . . . all apparently require many supplies (the aforementioned snacks, underwear, and wallet spring to mind) that a handy mom or dad is expected to carry. Change it up by wearing a fanny pack and you've just fulfilled the requirements of #4 as well. How low will you go?
- *Wine carrier:* Ooops, that should have read "whine carrier." Theory: If a child whines and there is no parental response, the whining escalates to a full-blown tantrum. Why not also give him three quarters so he can get an extra gum ball to shove in that gaping maw?
- *Sit and ride (mostly for the dads):* The ever-popular shoulder ride with all its inherent risks (hair pulling, eyeglass-frame twisting, booger dropping, and other more fluid bodily expulsions). Every baby and toddler loves this. My advice is, don't give the first ride, ever. Or just go all the way and get that frigging babywearer.

As much as a "fun belt" can really "jazz up" an outfit (holy shit! I have so turned into my mother!), a child can manage to "slum down" any snappy outfit you might have managed to put together. Really, the *only* way a child can be seen as an accessory is one gone terribly wrong. Having children can cause normally fashion-conscious adults to wear sloppy corporate-logoed sweatshirts, high-waisted mom jeans, sensible running shoes, sandals with socks (so bad it's worth mentioning twice), even fleece pants. If we truly are to embrace the child as accessory theory, I'm a little bit worried. With four children, I'm likely overaccessorized. I probably still have an extra diaper or two in my house just in case the 4-year-old has a relapse.

Tags: Mom Jeans. Fleece. Need I Say More.

December 3
Truth Be Told

"If you keep making that face it will stay that way!"

As soon as the words were out of my mouth I knew a) I was channelling my parents and b) there was nothing I could do to help myself. Mind games with children come naturally to parents (Hellooo? Santa, the Easter Bunny, the flipping Tooth Fairy?). And remember reverse psychology? It's a classic, and still deployed with great success today. Here's how it works. It is totally okay to tell your child that he will never again be allowed to eat broccoli, sleep in his own bed, or call his sister anything but butthead. Yes, you're tricking him. Yes, he'll fall for it (at least the first time), and *no*, these harmless lies and secrets won't send him to the psychiatrist's couch. Your insistence on telling the truth at all costs and "treating him with respect and dignity" will do that.

Tags: Manipulation. Fun.

December 25
Christmas Day

Here I am, celebrating the joyous birth of the beloved and precious one. The only one. Yep, it's a year today since I first laid thumbs on my little electronic friend. It's been a good year—we've had our ups and downs, our outages and our outrages, but mostly . . . we've had each other. And as I sneak away to write this holiday entry, I'm inspired by various traditional Christmas songs that I'd like to share with you, BB style:

- We Three Rings
- God Rest Ye Berry Gentlemen
- We Wish You a Berry Christmas (of course!)
- Oh Hum, All Ye Faithful
- Rudolph the Red-Flashing-Light-Message-Waiting Reindeer

And mostly, yes, Victoria, you did see Mommy Kissing Seamus.

Tags: BB's first Christmas. Awwww.

December 30
How It's All Coming Together in a Ganging Up Sort of Way

Let me start with a short anecdote. Yesterday I heard the words no mother ever wants to hear—*particularly* about her teenage daughter, and *especially* coming from a middle-aged slightly suspicious-looking man.

> "Ms. Buckworth?"
> "Um, yes?"
> "You have a daughter named Victoria?"
> "Why?"
> "I have her listed on your account. Great news. She's eligible for her own BlackBerry smartphone!"

It was at this point in the conversation that I used that very professional parenting technique of covering my ears and singing, "Lla la la la la I can't hear you." Can you imagine? A teenaged girl with a BB? A teenage girl who's not Paris Hilton or Lindsay Lohan? No thanks! I'm actually not worried about my daughter communicating with her buddies in the middle of school (she has a cellphone for that). It's the potential for cyber-nagging that really worries me. No, not me nagging her—the other way around. (Those of you with teenaged daughters will totally get this point.)

Subject: Shopping—URGENT!

Text: I *need* to go to American Eagle. Check your online calendar now.

Subject: Form—URGENT!
Text: I forgot the form for the rock-climbing class. It starts in five minutes. Bring it now, and don't forget the $25 fee.

Subject: Your son—URGENT!
Text: I just saw your son (my stupid brother) walking toward the principal's office.

Subject: Babysitting—URGENT!
Text: I can't babysit for your friend tonight because there's a field hockey game. Just tell her to drop the kids at our house instead. You're not doing anything.

Subject: OMG—URGENT!
Text: My friends told me they saw you wearing those low-rider jeans again. *Mom*!

Nagging is truly the domain of women, I get that (even in the teenage years). Men just don't care about things enough to bug someone else about them. They don't like talking about day-to-day domestic duties and they like arguing about them even less. The nagging gene is embedded in women early, and the convergence of technology and a woman's nagging voice is well established. Think about your voice-message lady (yes, dammit, I'm still here and I'll get back to you in a minute), the voice in your car that tells you a door is ajar (and a door is not a *jar*, duh), and basically any customer service line you call into—except, paradoxically, the technology companies. They always have a male voice. Trust me on this one.

There's maybe only one thing scarier than a teenager who is hooked on technology: that's a preschooler who's embedded in it. Yes, the parallel universes of toddlers and technology have finally merged into a phenomenon more frightening than my good friend's 30-plus-piece collection of unblinking Sleepytime Dolls: the dreaded Webkinz, otherwise known as crack for kids.

For months our household managed to remain sheltered from this terrifying invasion. But then came the inevitable birthday party, followed by the predictable breakdown after school one day ("But Mom, everyone has one!"). This led to my frantic chase across the city one windy and rainy night to find this elusive marvel of technology at its best—whose earthly form is a stuffed animal. I kid you not. Chad the Dalmatian and Chester the Beagle have single-handedly taken over my office computer (in fact, I had to push their "adoption" certificates out of the way before I could write this entry). The need to virtually "play" with them has turned my youngest kids into zombified children-of-the-corn freaks. I have actually been asked to feed the "dogs" while the children are "forced" to be away at school. If I ever catch myself doing this I will truly have gone to the dark side. Do not resuscitate me for any reason.

The only benefit of this technology (and its predecessor, Nintendogs, which did not include a real stuffed toy, but kept the cyberdogs locked inside a small screen) is that it may dispel the need to own a real pet. If only I'd known about this before I decided to bring four real children into the world! I could have become the Angelina Jolie of the virtual child adoption world.

Despite this Webkinz craze, there are some times when technology and toddlers can work together. Any BB-carrying

Mom can tell you that the hours spent sitting on the floor building wooden train sets, building block towers, and creating simply fantastic homemade Valentine's cards pass infinitely more quickly if one is able to simultaneously read and answer emails. The problem is, the little buggers (the children, not the BlackBerry) want not only your physical presence, but also your *attention* (greedy brats). The mom who tries to sneak a peak as the glue is drying under the lacy heart covered with sequins can expect cries of "Mom! If you don't put your BlackBerry away I'm going to throw it in the toilet!" I have tried to explain to my 4-year-old that I can multi-task, and am quite capable of emailing while facing the demanding challenges of putting a Thomas the Tank Engine track together (unlike his father). Somehow, though, I always manage to get caught when he asks either a lame-ass or insightful question, and I answer with a mindless "uh huh." This can be met with "You mean, I really *can* have 14 cookies for lunch?"

My solution? Get them hooked on their own portable technology. A handheld gaming unit can be a lifesaver when stuck in a doctor's office, in line for those blasted "must have" swimming lessons, or just when you're trying to read the frigging paper for five minutes. There is, of course, a downside. Your children, too, will soon exhibit the same addiction to their technology, and when you're trying to get them out the front door, to eat their dinner, or get ready for bed, you'll find *yourself* saying, "If you don't put that down right now, I'm throwing it in the toilet!"

Tags: Convergence. Technology. Children. Bliss.